TAKE OFF 1

ARBEITSBUCH

Cornelsen & Oxford University Press

Inhaltsverzeichnis

Unit 0	**My name is ...**	Seite 1
Unit 1	**Nice to meet you**	Seite 5
Unit 2	**How to get there**	Seite 9
Unit 3	**Shopping**	Seite 15
Unit 4	**Time and date**	Seite 22
Unit 5	**Invitations**	Seite 31
Stop Over	**Test 1**	Seite 37
Unit 6	**Every day ...**	Seite 42
Unit 7	**Travelling in Britain**	Seite 49
Unit 8	**Food and drink**	Seite 54
Unit 9	**Talking about the past**	Seite 59
Unit 10	**What's the matter?**	Seite 65
Stop Over	**Test 2**	Seite 70
Schlüssel		Seite 77
Inhaltsverzeichnis der Übungsinhalte		Seite 89

Wie arbeite ich zu Hause?

1. „Wie kann ich wiederholen, was in der Stunde durchgenommen wurde?"

    - Lesen Sie sich die **Übungen im Lehrbuch** noch einmal durch,
    - schlagen Sie die Vokabeln nach, die Sie vergessen haben,
    - sehen Sie sich die **Grammatikregeln** neben der Übung an und schlagen Sie unter der angegebenen Ziffer in der Anhangsgrammatik nach, in welchem größeren Zusammenhang die Regel steht (z. B. ▷ G 6.2 (a)).
    - Lernen Sie die neuen **Vokabeln** so, wie es auf S. 118 im Lehrbuch empfohlen wird.
    - Arbeiten Sie jetzt nach Möglichkeit mit der **Übungscassette**: dort finden Sie zu den allermeisten Übungen des Lehrbuchs einfache Nachsprech- und Grammatikübungen sowie kleinere Hörszenen, bei denen Sie eine Rolle übernehmen sollen: so können Sie den neuen Stoff Schritt für Schritt einüben (Verweis ▷ CC).
    - Bearbeiten Sie dann die Übung im **Arbeitsbuch**, auf die von der Lehrbuchübung aus verwiesen wird (z. B.: ▷ AB 2 = Übung Nr. 2 in der entsprechenden Unit im Arbeitsbuch).
    Kontrollieren Sie die Lösungen mit dem Schlüssel im Anhang des Arbeitsbuchs: **wenn es Probleme gegeben hat, fragen Sie in der nächsten Sitzung Ihre/n Kursleiter/in.**

2. „Was tue ich, wenn ich einmal eine oder ein paar Sitzungen versäumt habe?"

    - Rufen Sie eine/n Teilnehmer/in an, lassen Sie sich sagen, was durchgenommen wurde; verabreden Sie sich nach Möglichkeit, um den versäumten Stoff gemeinsam durchzuarbeiten.
    - Gehen Sie bei der Aufarbeitung aber genauso vor, wie unter Punkt 1. beschrieben wurde.
    - Fragen Sie in der nächsten Sitzung unbedingt Ihre/n Kursleiter/in, was Sie genau nacharbeiten müssen; vielleicht hat er/sie ein paar Minuten Zeit für Sie, um bei offen gebliebenen Problemen zu helfen.

    Die Texte der Hörübungen (= Cassettensymbol 🎞 neben der Übungsnummer) finden Sie übrigens im Anhang des Lehrbuchs auf S. 142, falls Sie die Hörcassette nicht besitzen.

3. „Wann und wie oft sollte man üben?"

    3–4 mal pro Woche 15–20 Minuten! Die Cassetten kann man auch nebenbei immer wieder laufen lassen (im Auto auf dem Weg zur Arbeit, bei der Hausarbeit, auf dem Walkman in der Straßenbahn): auch dabei prägen sich Redewendungen ein. Daneben: Wiederholen Sie auch einmal länger zurückliegenden Stoff – Nachlesen genügt, wenn man es regelmäßig tut. Und: immer wieder die Wörter lernen – dann fällt das Gespräch im Unterricht mit den anderen Teilnehmern sicher leichter.

4. „Und wenn ich etwas vergessen habe?"

    Machen Sie sich mit den **Nachschlagemöglichkeiten** im Lehrwerk vertraut! Ihr/e Kursleiter/in hilft Ihnen sicher dabei. Wörter, die man vergessen hat, findet man mit Hilfe der **Alphabetischen Wortliste** (S. 140); Grammatik schlägt man in der **Anhangsgrammatik** nach (– die übrigens auch ein **Inhaltsverzeichnis** und **Begriffserklärungen** enthält). Machen Sie sich auch mit der **Lautschrift** vertraut (Erklärung auf der hinteren inneren Umschlagseite des Lehrbuchs) – dann können Sie im Vokabelteil auch einmal überprüfen, ob Sie ein weniger vertrautes Wort richtig aussprechen.

5. „Soll ich mich auf Stunden vorbereiten?"

    Eigentlich nicht. Ihr/e Kursleiter/in gibt sich große Mühe, den neuen Stoff in leicht verständlicher Form einzuführen. Da er/sie besser weiß, welche Art der Erklärung gerade Ihnen und Ihrem Kurs am leichtesten fällt, sollten Sie besser nicht „vorlernen". So vermeiden Sie auch die Gefahr, daß Sie etwas Falsches lernen (z. B. eine falsche Aussprache, wenn Sie die Lautschrift nicht kennen). Stellen Sie lieber Fragen, wenn Sie etwas nicht gleich verstehen: Nicht nur durch Fehler, sondern vor allem auch durch Fragen wird man klug! Aber: eine Stunde **nachzubereiten** – den Stoff gründlich **zu wiederholen** und sich einzuprägen, ist immer sinnvoll, weil man dann den neuen Stoff, der ja an den alten anknüpft, viel leichter versteht.

Vorwort

6. „Braucht man unbedingt die Übungscassetten?"

Nicht unbedingt, vor allem dann nicht, wenn Sie ohnehin im Sprachlabor arbeiten können, oder wenn die Cassetten regelmäßig im Unterricht eingesetzt werden. Sie helfen aber viel, weil gerade Erwachsene sehr viel genauer hinhören müssen als Kinder, um eine neue Sprache zu lernen, und weil man im Unterricht halt doch nicht so oft drankommt, wie es eigentlich gut wäre. Und Regellernen und grammatisches Wissen alleine genügt nicht – man muß immer auch sein ‚**Können**' üben. (Ein Tip: Vielleicht gibt es die Cassetten ja auch in einer öffentlichen Bibliothek zur Ausleihe?)

7. „Lesen und Schreiben"

Die **Lesetexte** im Lehrbuch und im Arbeitsbuch sollten Sie so benutzen, wie Sie Texte auch in Ihrer Muttersprache behandeln: Lesen Sie sie zur Unterhaltung, um ihnen eine Information zu entnehmen, aus ‚landeskundlichem' Interesse. **Schlagen Sie nicht jedes einzelne Wort nach,** das Sie nicht sofort verstehen (bedenken Sie, was im Vorwort des Lehrbuchs „So arbeiten Sie mit Take Off" unter „Leseverständnis" sowie auf S. 17 steht). Sie haben dann viel mehr Freude daran. **Schreiben** werden Sie vor allem dann üben wollen, wenn Sie Englisch aus beruflichen Gründen lernen, wenn Sie die Hausaufgaben Ihrer Kinder nachsehen wollen usw. Falls Ihnen die Übungen im Arbeitsbuch und die gelegentlichen Schreibanlässe im Lehrbuch nicht genügen, sprechen Sie einmal mit Ihrer Kursleiterin/Ihrem Kursleiter darüber. Wenn Sie um mehr Schreibaufgaben und um Korrektur Ihrer Arbeit bitten, bedenken Sie aber, daß sie/er oft nur nebenberuflich tätig ist und deshalb vielleicht nur wenig Zeit für Korrekturen hat. Vielleicht können Sie aber auch eine **gegenseitige Korrekturhilfe im Kurs** organisieren.

8. „Und dieses Arbeitsbuch?"

Es enthält – wenn Sie alle Übungen, auf die im Anschluß an eine Lehrbuchübung verwiesen wird, bearbeitet haben – eine Reihe von **zusammenfassenden Übungen zu Wortschatz und Redewendungen**, dazu auch in jeder Unit zusätzliche Leseaufgaben, Rätsel usw. Bearbeiten Sie diese Dinge jeweils **am Ende einer Unit. Schlagen Sie bei allen Übungen niemals im Lösungsschlüssel nach, bevor Sie alle Bearbeitungshilfen** (z. B. in den Kästen über der Übung) **ausgeschöpft** und die Grammatik im Lehrbuch zu Rate gezogen haben.

Viel Spaß nicht nur bei der Arbeit im Kurs, sondern auch beim Lernen zu Hause,

wünschen Ihnen

Verlag und Autoren.

Unit 0 My name is...

1 Wie man seinen Namen sagt und nach Namen fragt

Kurzform	Langform
I'm	I am

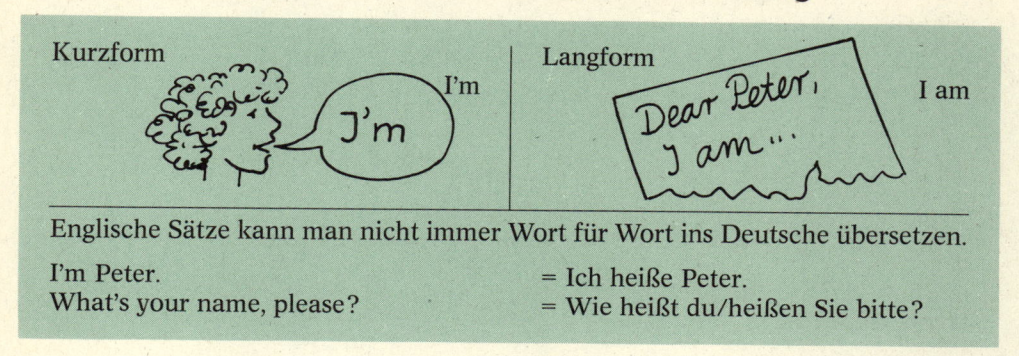

Englische Sätze kann man nicht immer Wort für Wort ins Deutsche übersetzen.

I'm Peter. = Ich heiße Peter.
What's your name, please? = Wie heißt du/heißen Sie bitte?

1 *Vervollständigen Sie die Fragen der Hotelangestellten.*

– _What's your name_, please?

– Barker.

– And _what's your_ first name

(= *Vorname*), _please_ ?

– Anthony.

2 *Die Mädchen sagen, wie sie heißen.*

– _I'm Mary_.
– _I'm Julie_.
– _I'm Debbie_.

3 *Die Sekretärin will wissen, wie der Gesprächspartner heißt.*

– _What's your name, please_ ?

4 *Der Schloßführer stellt sich Ihnen vor.*

– Hello. _I'm_ Peter.
What's your _name, please?_

Unit 0 – My name is ...

2 Wie man **this** und **that** benutzt

*Setzen Sie **this** oder **that** ein.*

– Is ___this___¹ Angela Brown?

– ___that___'s⁴ Oliver White, my English teacher.

– I'm John and ___this___² is Nancy.
– Hello, John. Hello, Nancy.
  I'm Eric and ___this___³ is Jim.

3 Wie man jemanden begrüßt

Ordnen Sie die Begrüßungen den Bildern zu.

ungezwungen: **Hi/Hello**
förmlich: **Good morning/evening**

1 ___Hi___   2 ___Good morning___

3 ___Hello___   4 _____

   a – Good morning, Mr Parker.   b – Hello, Tom!   c – Good morning, Mr Brown.   d – Hi, Linda!
       – Good morning, Linda.   – Hello, Jack!   – Good morning, Simpson.   – Hi!

Unit 0 – My name is . . .

4 Wie man sich nach dem Befinden erkundigt, und wie man auf solche Fragen antwortet

> – How are you?   – Fine, thanks.
>   I'm fine, thank you.
>   Not so bad.

Ergänzen Sie bitte folgende Dialoge.

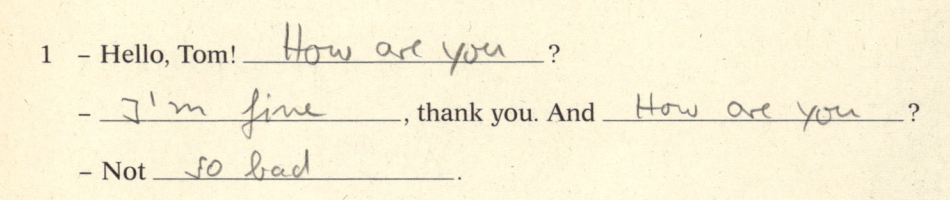

1 – Hello, Tom! __How are you__ ?
   – __I'm fine__ , thank you. And __How are you__ ?
   – Not __so bad__ .

2 – Good morning, Mrs Brown.
   – Good morning, Dave. __How are you__ ?
   – __I'm fine__ , __thank you__ .

3 – Hi, Jack! __How are you__ today?
   – Oh, not __so bad__ . And you?
   – __Fine__ , thanks.

5 Wie man am, are und is benutzen kann

> (a) Die Grundbedeutung von I **am**   ist   ich **bin**
>   you **are**   du **bist**
>   Tom **is**   Tom **ist**
>   my friends **are**   meine Freunde **sind**
>
> (b) **Am**, **are** und **is** werden weiterhin zum Ausdruck des Befindens benutzt.
>   – How **is** Peter?   – He's fine, thank you.

Mit welcher Bedeutung (a) oder (b) werden am, are und is hier benutzt?

(b) 1 – Hi, Rose. How **are** you today?   __Befinden__
    2 – This **is** Peter and that's his friend.   __ist__
    3 – Some of my best friends **are** teachers.   __sind__
    4 – Pat **is** a name for a girl.   __ist__
(b) 5 – How **are** your friends? – Fine, thanks.   __Befinden__
    6 – I'**m** Peter's friend.   __bin__

Unit 0 – My name is . . .

6 *Versuchen Sie, dieses Vokabelrätsel durch Ergänzen der englischen Sätze auszufüllen. Nr. 10 muß senkrecht ausgefüllt werden und dient als Kontrolle.*

1. HELLO
2. GOODBYE
3. WHAT
4. TEACHER
5. GIRL
6. NAME
7. MARY
8. FLOWER
9. YOUR

1 – . . . , Peter!
2 . . . , Pat. See you next week.
3 . . . 's your name?
4 Mr Green is my English . . . .
5 Iris is a name for a . . . .
6 – What's your . . . ?
   – My name's Alf Berg.
7 . . . is a name for a girl.
8 Violet is a name for a girl and a . . . .
9 Is Mr Berg . . . English teacher?
10 – . . . ?
   – I'm fine, thank you.

7 Rätsel zu englischen Wörtern, die auch im Deutschen benutzt werden

Ergänzen Sie die fehlenden Buchstaben.

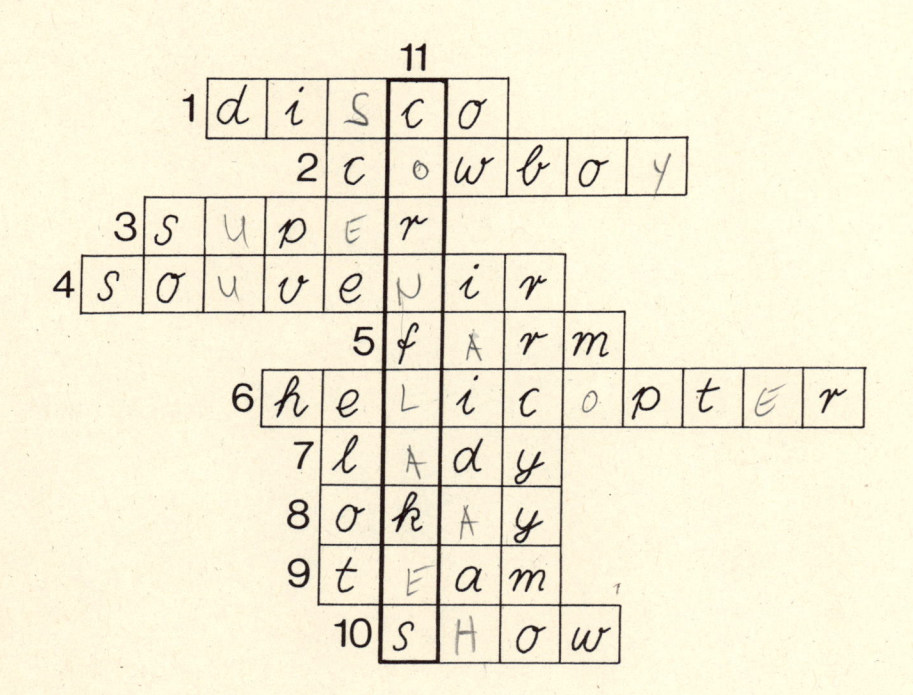

1. disco
2. cowboy
3. super
4. souvenir
5. farm
6. helicopter
7. lady
8. okay
9. team
10. show

Unit 1 Nice to meet you

1 Wie man nach der Herkunft fragt, und wie man auf solche Fragen antwortet

- Where are you from? – I'm from ...
- Where is | John | from? – | John | 's from ...
           | Rose | – | Sue |
           | it | – | It |

① Where are you from?

I'm from Kuwait.

It's from Ireland.

② Where is it from?

③ Where's your friend from?

Peter is from Bristol.

2 A or (= oder) an?

| an (a... e... i... o... u... | a | b... c... d... f... ... |

*Fill in (= setzen Sie ein) **a** or **an**.*

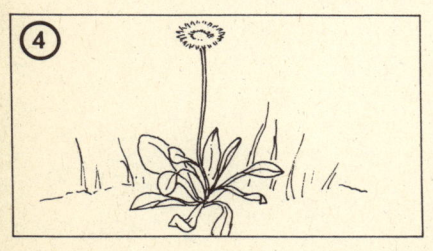

1 This is __a__ Ferrari. It's __an__ Italian car.

2 This is __an__ old village. It's __a__ village in England.

3 This is Tom, __an__ English teacher from Canada. He's from __a__ town near Montreal.

4 This is __a__ daisy. „Daisy" is __an__ English name for __a__ flower.

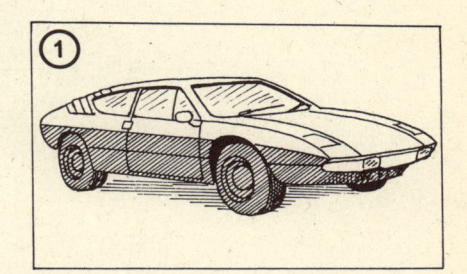

Unit 1 – Nice to meet you

3 Wie man auf Ja/Nein-Fragen antwortet

> – Is . . . ?   – Yes, it is.
>   – No, it isn't. (= is not)
>
> Nur mit **Yes** oder **No** zu antworten klingt oft unhöflich oder schroff.

Answer (= Antworten Sie), please.

1 – Is *Iris* an English name? – _____, _____.
2 – Is Toronto a city in the United States? – _No_, _it isn't_.
3 – Is your first name *Daisy*? – _No_, _it isn't_.
4 – Is Offenbach near Frankfurt? – _Yes_, _it is_.
5 – Is *Renate* a German name? – _Yes_, _it is_.

4 Wie man Auskünfte über sich selbst gibt

Die Studenten der englischen Sprachschule fragen nach dem Namen, dem Beruf und der Herkunft und antworten einander. Vervollständigen Sie die Fragen und Antworten.

a – _Are_ you Pierre Jardin?
– No, _I'm not, I'm_ Peter Hummel.
– _Where do you come_ from, Peter?
– _I come from_ Freiburg in Germany, but I _live_ in Hamburg now.
– _What's_ your job?
– I _work_ in a hotel. I'_m_ a waiter.

b – _Are you_ Maria?
– Yes, _I'm_.
– _Where are you_ from, Maria?
– _I come_ from Basel in Switzerland, but I _live_ in Bern now.
– _Are you_ a student?
– No, _I'm not_. _I'm_ a secretary. I _work_ in a hotel.

Unit 1 – Nice to meet you

5 Wie man nach dem Befinden fragt, und was man bei einer förmlichen Vorstellung sagt

Fill in (= Setzen Sie ein)
How are you? *or* ***How do you do.***

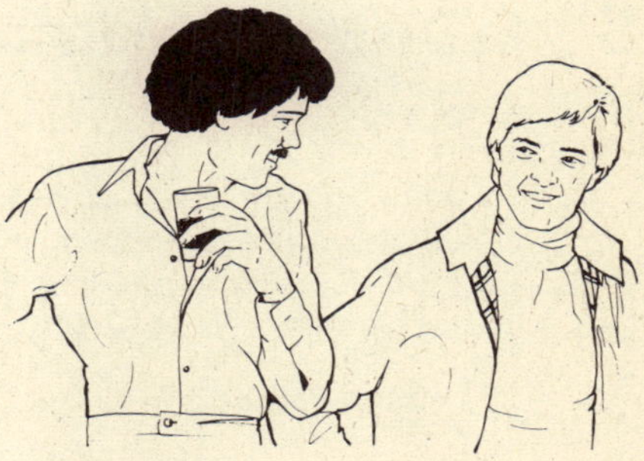

1. How are you?
2. How do you do? 
3. How are you?
4. How are you? 
5. How do you do? 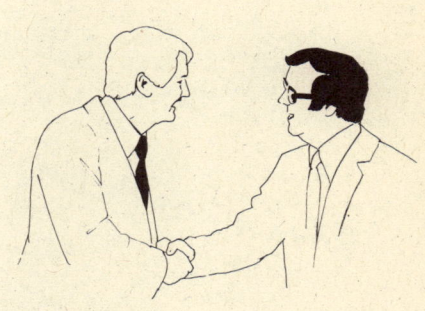

Fine, thanks, and you?

6 Wie man Informationen über sich bzw. eine andere Person weitergibt

über sich selbst	über eine andere (= 3.) Person
I'm	Tom/he/she **is** ....
I live	Susan/he/she live**s** ....

Fill in: ***are, is, 'm, live, lives, work, works***

1. John Clark __is__ an English teacher. He __comes__ from a town near New York but he __lives__ in Germany now. He __works__ at the Volkshochschule in Heidelberg.
2. I __'m__ from Frankfurt and my friend Alf __is__ from a village near Frankfurt.
   I __live__ in Hamburg now and Alf __lives__ in Berlin.
   I __work__ in an office and he __works__ in a hotel.

Unit 1 – Nice to meet you

7 Wo man die s-Endung benutzt

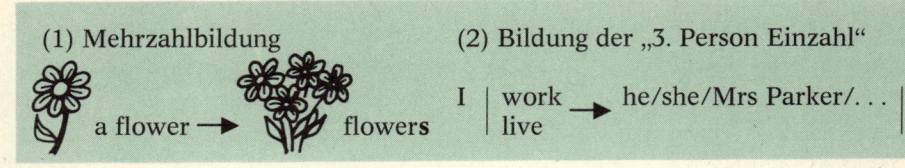

(1) Mehrzahlbildung a flower → flowerS

(2) Bildung der „3. Person Einzahl"
I work / live → he/she/Mrs Parker/... works / liveS

Fügen Sie nur dort, wo es notwendig ist, ein „s" hinzu.

1 – Some _ of _ my _ best _ friend**s** _ are _ flower **s**.

2 – Jim _ live**s** _ in _ London _ and _ he _ work**s** _ in _ London _, too _.

3 – Iris _ and _ Daisy _ are _ name**s** _ for _ flower**s** and _ girl**s** _ in _ England _.

4 – I _ work _ in _ a _ factory _ and _ Susan _ work**s** in _ an _ office _.

5 – You _ are _ my _ best _ friend _, Tom _.

8 Länder, Nationalitäten und Berufe

In den Buchstaben sind 10 Wörter versteckt, die zu den obengenannten Wortfeldern passen. Manche Wörter müssen waagerecht und andere senkrecht gelesen werden. Umranden Sie die gefundenen Wörter.

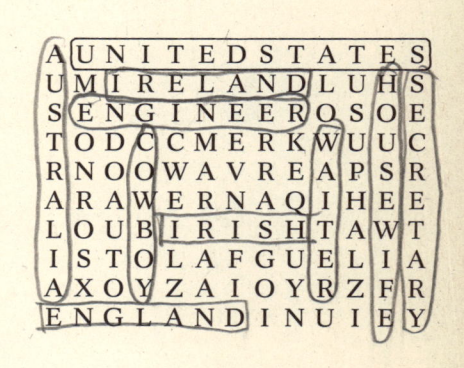

```
A U N I T E D S T A T E S
U M I R E L A N D L U H S
S E N G I N E E R O S O E
T O D C C M E R K W U U C
R N O O W A V R E A P S R
A R A W E R N A Q I H E E
L O U B I R I S H T A W T
I S T O L A F G U E L I A
A X O Y Z A I O Y R Z F R
E N G L A N D I N U I E Y
```

9

Versuchen Sie, das Anmeldeformular auszufüllen. Die unbekannten Wörter können Sie bestimmt erraten. Im Zweifelsfalle fragen Sie bitte Ihren Kursleiter/Ihre Kursleiterin.

Brentwood's Holiday Houses
REGISTRATION FORM
SURNAME: Walters   FIRST NAME: Barbara
ADDRESS: 315 Willington Ave, Kingston/Ontario
TELEPHONE NUMBER: 5496334   NATIONALITY: Canadian   OCCUPATION: secretary
AGE: 31   SEX: MALE ☐ FEMALE ☒

And this is for you:

Brentwood's Holiday Houses
REGISTRATION FORM
SURNAME: Fröhlich   FIRST NAME: Evgard
ADDRESS: Billtalstr. 13
TELEPHONE NUMBER: 06196/73680   NATIONALITY: german   OCCUPATION: secretary
AGE: 27   SEX: MALE ☐ FEMALE ☒

10

Schreiben Sie einem neuen englischen Brieffreund,

1 *woher Sie kommen,*
2 *wo Sie jetzt leben,*
3 *wo Sie arbeiten,*
  und fragen Sie ihn,
4 *woher er kommt und welchen Beruf er hat.*

I'm from Brück, and I live in Rosbach now. I work in the Deutsche Bundesbk. Where are you from? What's your job?

Unit 2 How to get there

1 Wie man nach der Anzahl fragt

> – How many ... **s are** there?
> – There **is** (only) **one**.   **Einzahl**
> – There **are two, three**/... / **none**. **Mehrzahl**

Fragen Sie nach der Anzahl, und antworten Sie nach den in Klammern gegebenen Vorgaben. Schreiben Sie die Zahlen bitte aus.

1 – _How many_ shops _are_ in your village?
  – _There are four_ (4).

2 – _How many_ hotels _are_ in your village?
  – _There is only one_ (1).

3 – _How many_ supermarkets _are_ in your village?
  – _There are two_ (2).

4 – _How many_ factories _are_ in your village?
  – _There are none_ (–).

2 Wie man Zugehörigkeit ausdrückt

> my, your, his, her

*Fill in **her** (1 x), **his** (1 x), **my** (2 x) and **your** (1 x).*

1 – Is your telephone number 6055?   – No, it isn't. _My_ telephone number is 66055.
2 – Is this Cindy's office?   – No, it isn't. _Her_ office is in King Street.
3 – Is this Eric's car?   – No, it isn't. _His_ car is near the supermarket.
4 – Is this _your_ car?   – No, it isn't. That's my car, the Volkswagen.
5 – Is this your key?   – No, it isn't. _My_ key is in the car.

3 Was man am Anfang eines Telefongesprächs sagt

*Entscheiden Sie, ob es sich um Sätze **(a)** des Anrufers oder **(b)** des Angerufenen handelt.*

1 – Hello, is that John speaking?   _a)_
2 – Sorry, wrong number.   _a)_
3 – Mirabelle Hotel. Good evening.   _b)_
4 – 335 022.   _b)_
5 – Dr Brown's office. Good morning.   _b)_
6 – Is that 332 156?   _a)_
7 – Yes, speaking.   _b)_
8 – Fred Jones speaking.   _a)_
9 – Good morning, Mr Sears. This is Ann Williams. _a)_

Unit 2 – How to get there

4 Wie man die Zugehörigkeit zu einer Person und einer Sache bezeichnet

Tom's room

the key **of** the room

1 What's the _name of the town_ ?
   (town – name)

2 The _guest's name_ is Greene.
   (guest – name)

3 _Mr. Simpson's office_ is near the supermarket.
   (Mr Simpson – office)

4 The _telephone number of the Westminster Bank_ is 3359.
   (Westminster Bank – telephone number)

5 _Peter's nationality_ is German.
   (Peter – nationality)

6 The _manager of the ABC Supermarket_ is Mr Sherwood.
   (the ABC Supermarket – manager)

7 _Ann's room_ is near my room.
   (Ann – room)

8 _Cindy's telephone number_ is not in the directory.
   (telephone number – Cindy)

9 This is a very old _directory of Oxford_.
   (directory – Oxford)

5 Wie man Zahlen schreibt

fifteen   eighty   thirty   eighteen
four   ninety-nine   forty-four
ninety   three   nineteen   fifty

Ordnen Sie die ausgeschriebenen Zahlen im Kasten den Ziffern zu. Schreiben Sie dann auch die übrigen Zahlen aus.

4 _four_	8 _eight_	9 _nine_
14 _fourteen_	18 _eighteen_	19 _nineteen_
44 _forty-four_	80 _eighty_	90 _ninety_
5 _five_	3 _three_	99 _ninety-nine_
15 _fifteen_	13 _thirteen_	
50 _fifty_	30 _thirty_	

Unit 2 – How to get there

6 Wie man **there** und **their** benutzt

> **There** und **their** haben die gleiche Aussprache.
>
> **Their** [= *ihr(e)*] bezeichnet Zugehörigkeit zu mehreren Personen.
> **There is/are** heißt *es gibt/da ist/sind*.

*Fill in **their** or **there**.*

1 _Their_ garden is very nice. _There_ are a lot of flowers in it.

2 _There_ are three supermarkets in this town.

3 _Their_ telephone number is 342 500.

4 What's _their_ address?

5 How many flowers are _there_ in Ziggy's garden?

6 _There_ is only one bank and _there_ are three factories in our village.

7 Wie man Auskunft auf die Frage nach dem Weg gibt

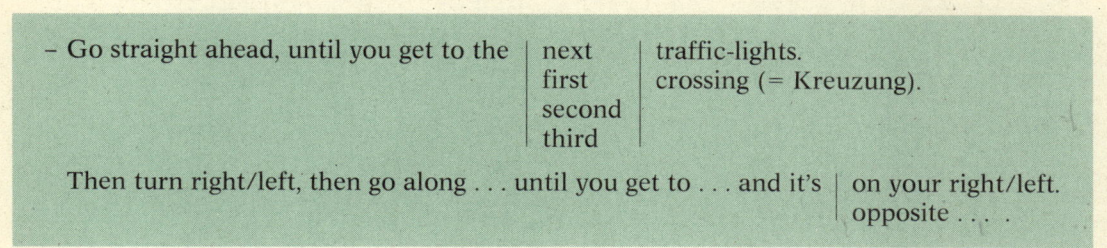

> – Go straight ahead, until you get to the | next | traffic-lights.
> | first | crossing (= Kreuzung).
> | second |
> | third |
>
> Then turn right/left, then go along ... until you get to ... and it's | on your right/left.
> | opposite ....

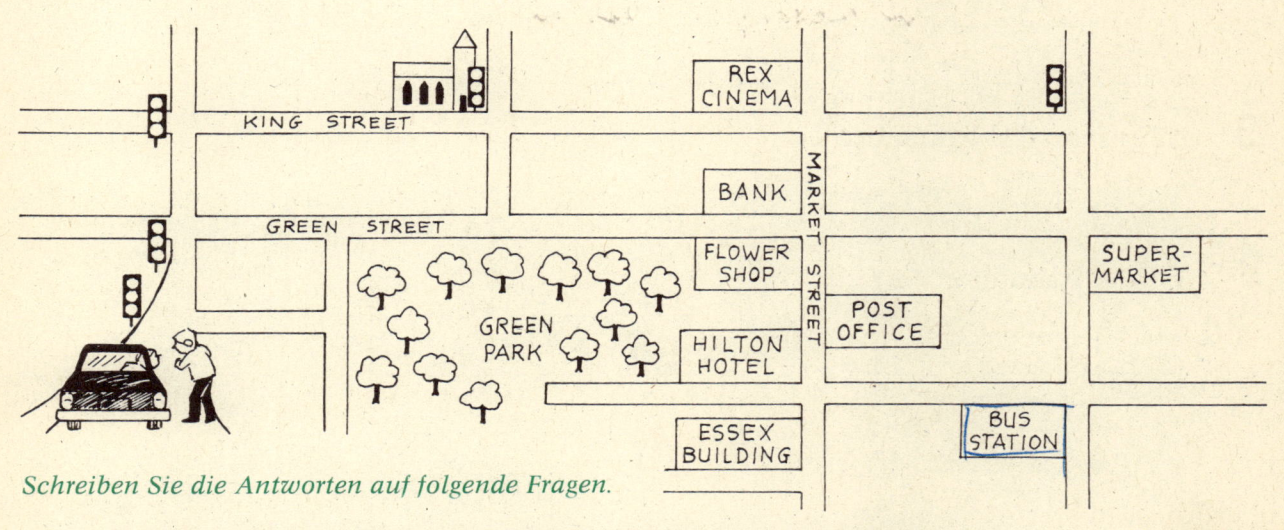

Schreiben Sie die Antworten auf folgende Fragen.

1 – Excuse me, can you tell me how to get to the nearest flower shop, please?

– Yes.

___
___
___
___

Unit 2 – How to get there

2 – Excuse me, can you tell me where the Rex Cinema is, please?

– Yes. Go straight ahead, until you get to the second crossing. Then turn right in King Street and go along until you get to the second crossing. There, on your left is the Rex Cinema.

3 – Excuse me, where's the nearest supermarket?

– Go straight ahead, until you get to the next crossing. Then turn right in the Green Street and go along until you get to the second crossing. The supermarket is opposite of it on the right.

4 – *Fragen Sie nach dem Hilton Hotel und antworten Sie.*

– Excuse me, can you tell me how to get to the Hilton Hotel, please?

– Yes, go straight ahead, until you get to the next crossing. Then turn right in Green Street and go along until you get to the first crossing. Then turn right in Market Street and go along until you get to the next crossing. There on your right is the Hilton Hotel.

8 Wortschatzrätsel

Crossword answers:
- 1 down: TELEPHONE
- 2 down: ADDRESS
- 3 down: FLOOR
- 4 down: CINEMA
- 5 down: STATION
- 6 down: EIGHT
- 7 across: TRAFFIC-LIGHTS
- 8 across: NINE
- 9 across: SIX
- 10 across: EIGHTY

Unit 2 – How to get there

KENT CARAVAN HIRE
SPECIALISTS IN "CONSTRUCTION SITE" CARAVANS AND CARAVAN TRANSPORTING
Chamber Wharf, Abbey Rd., Faversham, Kent.
PROPS. L. N. BROWN
L. J. RICHMAN
FAVERSHAM 5131 & 5132
AND COVERING WHOLE OF ENGLAND

Schauen Sie sich die Anzeige der Wohnwagenvermietung genau an und versuchen Sie, das Rätsel zu lösen.

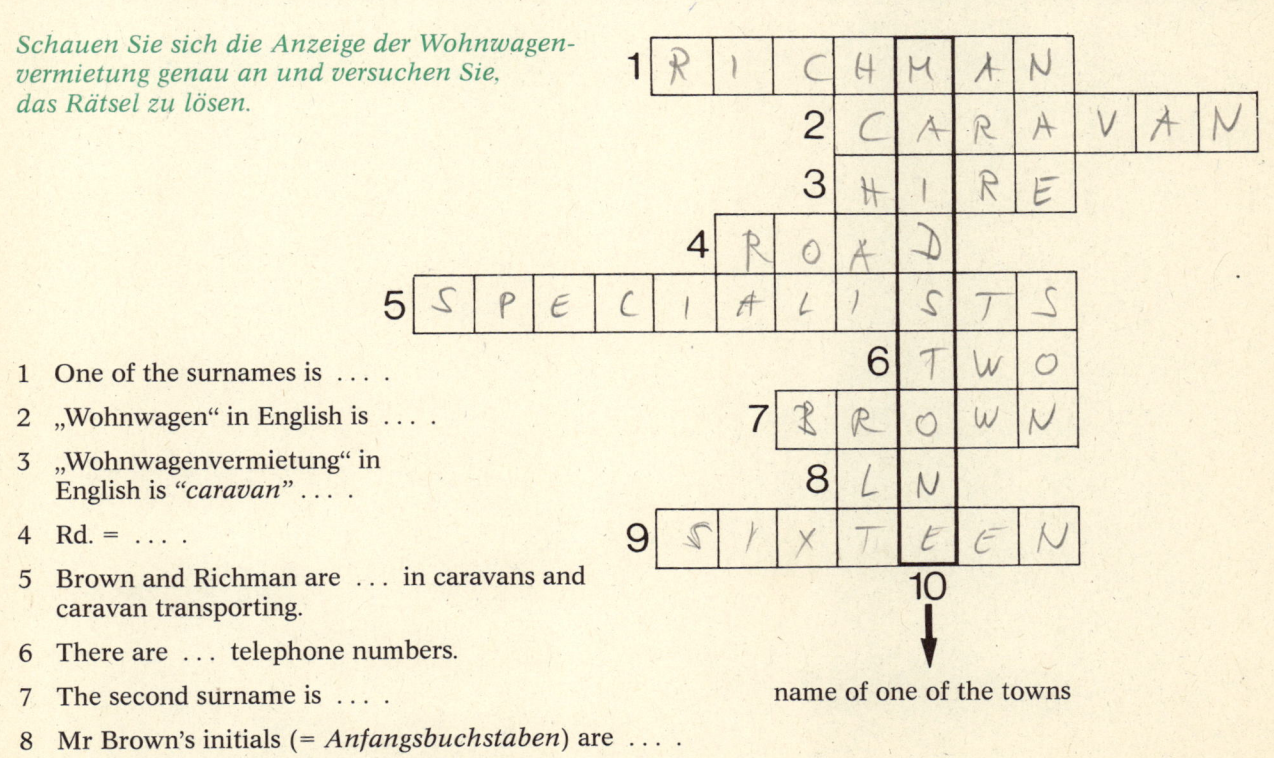

1. RICHMAN
2. CARAVAN
3. HIRE
4. ROAD
5. SPECIALISTS
6. TWO
7. BROWN
8. LN
9. SIXTEEN

10 ↓ name of one of the towns

1. One of the surnames is ....
2. „Wohnwagen" in English is ....
3. „Wohnwagenvermietung" in English is *"caravan"* ....
4. Rd. = ...
5. Brown and Richman are ... in caravans and caravan transporting.
6. There are ... telephone numbers.
7. The second surname is ....
8. Mr Brown's initials (= *Anfangsbuchstaben*) are ....
9. Kent Caravan Hire is in ... towns in Kent.

Unit 2 – How to get there

10 *Ein Engländer schreibt einem Bekannten den* **Namen**, *die* **Adresse** *und die* **Telefonnummer** *eines Arztes auf. Vervollständigen Sie die Notiz.*

His name is Dr Betterton.
His address is 48 Winstanley Rd
and the telephone number
is 2734.

Bernhardt Dr A.Jefferson, Sholden Hall.....................Deal 4666
Best Dr R.M, Mill Ho,High St,Queenborough.......Sheerness 2088
Betterton Dr B.W, 48 Winstanley Rd ....Sheerness 2734
Bhat Dr K.M.Surgery,
            52 East Court La,Gillingham...Medway 31364
Birch Dr R.G, 70 East St..........................Sittingbourne 23197

Unit 3 Shopping

1 Wie man ausdrückt, ob einem etwas gefällt

> This is/That's (a) | (very) nice .... lovely.

2 Wie man Zugehörigkeit zu Personen ausdrückt

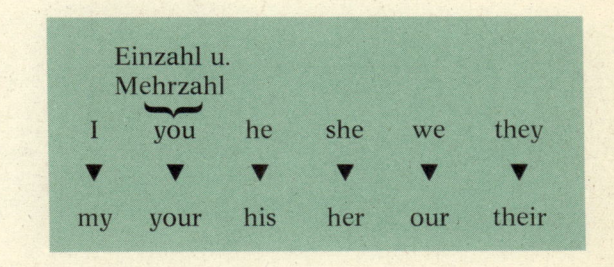

	Einzahl u. Mehrzahl				
I	you	he	she	we	they
▼	▼	▼	▼	▼	▼
my	your	his	her	our	their

Fill in I, my, ...

1 – Excuse me, can ___you___ tell me how

to get to Madison Avenue?

– Go straight ahead until ___you___ get to the

next crossing, and it's on ___your___ left.

– Thank you very much.

Unit 3 – Shopping

2

– Oh – isn't that Jim and _____ friend over there? _____ think _____'s from the States.

3 *Eine englische Familie beschreibt ein Photo mit ihrem deutschen Gast:*

– Here __we__ are in __our__ garden. That's Hans, __our__ German guest. __He__ is very nice, and __his__ English is very good.

Hans hat einen Abzug von dem Bild. Er sagt dazu:

– Here __I__ am in the garden of __my__ English family. __They__ live near Regent's Park. __They__ are very nice, and __their__ garden is beautiful.

3 Wie man fragt, wo man etwas bekommt

– Excuse me, | I'm looking for a . . . .
 | where can I/we get . . . s, please?

1 *Sie und Ihr/e Partner/in sind am Informationstisch eines Kaufhauses und wollen wissen, wo es Mäntel gibt.*

– Excuse me, we are looking for a coat _____?

2 *Sie sind auf der Straße und wollen wissen, wo es Regenschirme gibt.*

– _____?

3 *Sie suchen in einem Kaufhaus ein Paar Jeans. Sie fragen eine Verkäuferin.*

– _____.

Where _____?

4 Wie man Näheres und Ferneres bezeichnet

Unit 3 – Shopping

*Stellen Sie Fragen mit **this/that/these/those** und antworten Sie darauf.*

– Is this your coat?

① – No, it isn't. That's my coat.

– Do you want these records?

② – No, I want those.

– Is this your key?

③ – No, it isn't. That's my key.

– Is this your car?

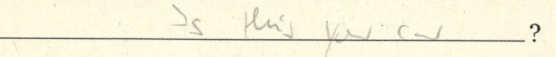

④ – No, it isn't. That's my car.

Unit 3 – Shopping

5 Wie man nach dem Preis fragt und darauf antwortet

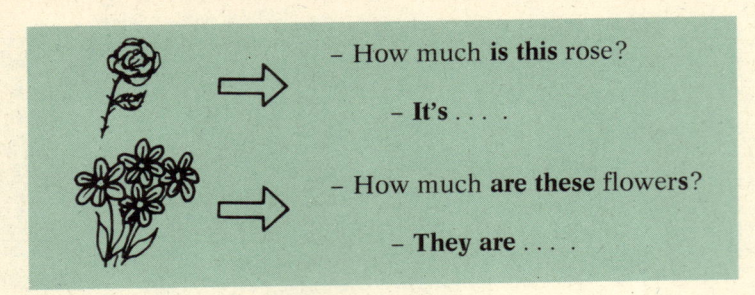

- How much **is this** rose?
- It's . . . .

- How much **are these** flower**s**?
- They are . . . .

Fragen Sie nach dem Preis der abgebildeten Dinge und geben Sie die Antworten.

1
– _____ home computer?
– _____ .

2
– _____ three records?
– _____ .

3
– _____ shoes?
– _____ .

4
– _____ ?
– _____ .

5
– _____ ?
– _____ .

Unit 3 – Shopping

6 Wie man **can** benutzen kann

> (a) can = Bitte: **Can** you . . . , **please**?
> can = (Un-)Fähigkeit: I **can (not)** speak English.
>
> (b) can't   cannot
>
> (c) he/she ▷ **can** write but he/she ▷ write**s**

*Bilden Sie mit Hilfe der Stichwörter Sätze mit **can** oder **can't**.*

1 You – get – telephone directories – in a department store.
   – _____.

2 I – have – your umbrella – please?
   – _____?

3 Your night school teacher – speak and write – English.
   – _____.

4 What – I – get – in that shop?
   – _____?

5 you – tell me – where – King Street – is – please?
   – _____?

6 We – get – T-shirts – in the department store in King Street.
   – _____.

7 The bank – change – notes – for you.
   – _____.

8 He – wear – that pullover, . . .
   – _____, it's not his size.

Unit 3 – Shopping

7 Things you can buy in a department store

1. SHOES
2. POSTER
3. FILM
4. CAMERA
5. SUITCASE
6. COAT
7. UMBRELLA
8. PULLOVER
9. BLOUSE
10. TROUSERS
11. DRESS
12. SHIRT

13. ↓

Unit 3 – Shopping

8 *Schauen Sie sich den Warenhauskatalog an und beantworten Sie die Fragen.*

1 – What can you see?

– I can see two _____, a _____ of _____, a _____

and four _____.

2 – Are these tennis shoes for girls?

– _____.

3 – What colour are the shoes?

– _____.

4 – Is this an American or an English T-shirt?

– _____.

5 – How much is the T-shirt?

– _____.

6 – Is 29 a big or a small size for jeans?

– _____.

7 – How much is one pair of these socks?

– _____.

8 – What is "save" in German?

– _____.

                                              deutsche Bezeichnungen

9 – You can get the T-shirt in S   (= small)   = _____.

                                   M (= medium) = _____.

                                   L   (= large)   = _____.

9 *Vervollständigen Sie den Briefausschnitt und fragen Sie nach dem **Preis** für **Jeans** und ein **Paar gute Schuhe**.*

> I like shopping in town but things are very *expencive*. Jeans are from *90* Marks to *150* Marks. A *pair of* shoes is 160 Marks. *How much is a pair of jeans* in your town? And *how much is a pair of good shoes* ?
> ....

Unit 4 Time and date

1 Wie man nach Öffnungszeiten fragt, und wie man auf solche Fragen antwortet

It's three o'clock.   It's half past three.

0.01 – 11.59   a. m. = in the morning
12.01 – 18.00 p. m. = in the afternoon
18.00 –   p. m. = in the evening

- When's the ... open?
- What time are the ... s open?

- It's open from ... to ... .
- They're open from ... in the morning till ... in the evening.

- Is the ... (still) open at/after ... o'clock?
- No, it isn't./Yes, it is.
  It's/They're open till ... .

Schreiben Sie die Uhrzeiten in dieser Übung so, wie sie gesprochen werden.

1 *Fragen Sie, wann das Restaurant geöffnet ist, und antworten Sie.*

Mourino's Restaurant
58 Porchester Road, London, W.2.
A corner of Spain in the heart of Paddington where the best Spanish food is served at a moderate price.
Open 7 days a week, 6–12 pm
RESERVATIONS: 01-727 9950

– _____?
– _____ midnight.

2
PLANETARIUM. Marylebone Road, NW1 (486 1121; adjacent to Baker Street tube). The Zeiss Star Projector takes you through space and time, there are Laser Light concerts and astronomers' exhibitions. Open daily from 11 am to 4.30 pm. Admission charge.

Fragen Sie, ob das Planetarium noch um 5 Uhr abends geöffnet ist, und antworten Sie.

– _____?
– _____.

3 Banking hours are 9.30 a. m. – 3.30 p. m.

Fragen Sie, ob die Bank noch offen ist (es ist 16.00), und antworten Sie.

– _____?
– _____
  _____.

Unit 4 – Time and date

4 *Fragen Sie nach der Öffnungszeit der Post in Dublin, und antworten Sie.*

> **Post Office hours**
> The General Post Office, O'Connell Street, Dublin, is open daily from 8.00 hrs. to 23.00 hrs. for sale of stamps and acceptance of telegrams, registered letters and express letters.

– _____ ?

– _____ at night (= *nachts*).

5 *Sagen Sie einem Engländer die Öffnungszeit Ihrer Bank.*

– _____

6 *Sagen Sie einem Engländer, wie lange die Post in Deutschland geöffnet hat.*

– _____

2 Wie man sagt, wie spät es ist

> volle Stunde
>
> 2) twenty-six minutes to nine (in the morning)
> 4) two minutes to two (in the afternoon)
> 6) five past one (in the afternoon)
> 11) a quarter to eight (in the evening)
> 3) twenty-nine minutes past eleven (in the morning)
> 8) twenty-six minutes past eight (in the morning)
> 9) twenty-nine minutes to twelve (in the morning)
> 7) five to one (in the afternoon)
> 10) 5) half past seven (in the evening)
>
> to = vor, bis   past = nach
>
> 30 minutes = **half past**; 15 minutes = **(a) quarter**

Ordnen Sie die im Kasten enthaltenen Uhrzeiten den abgebildeten Uhren zu; schreiben Sie dann auch die übrigen Zeiten aus.

19:45 1) _____
8:34   2) _____
11:29 3) _____
13.58 4) _____
19.30 5) _____
13:05 6) _____
12:55 7) _____
8:26   8) _____
11:31 9) _____
7:30 10) half past seven (in the morning)
18:45 11) a quarter to seven (in the evening)
14:02 12) two minuts past two (in the afternoon)

Unit 4 – Time and date

3 Wie man nach Abfahrts- und Ankunftszeiten fragt, und wie man auf solche Fragen antwortet

- What time are the trains to ...?   – There's one at ... and at ....
- Is there a train to ... in the | morning?
                                 | afternoon?

LONDON – INVERNESS			
King's Cross	dep	0800	1200
Inverness	arr	1730	2135
Inverness	dep	0830	1230
King's Cross	arr	1748	2238

Schreiben Sie die Uhrzeiten bei den Antworten in Ziffern.

1 *Sie möchten wissen, wann Züge nach Inverness fahren.*
 – What time are trains to Inverness ?
 – There's one at 8 o'clock in the morning and at noon

2 *Sie möchten wissen, ob nachmittags ein Zug nach Inverness fährt.*
 – Is there a train to Inverness in the afternoon ?
 – No, there isn't a train to Inverness in the afternoon.

3 *Sie möchten wissen, ob vormittags ein Zug nach London fährt.*
 – Is there a train to London in the morning ?
 – Yes, there's one at 8.30 in the morning.

4 Wie man Vorschläge macht, und wie man auf Vorschläge reagiert

to make a proposal / to propose s.th.

Vorschläge machen

Let's ....
Shall we ...?
We can/could ....

Auf Vorschläge reagieren

Can/Could you/we ... (instead)?
Well, I'm not really interested in ....
Yes, that's a good idea. (great)
Let's ... instead.

Fill in, please.

1 – The Tower is very interesting. __Shall we__ go there on Sunday?

   Not on Sunday. But __can we can__ go there on Monday or on Tuesday, when we've got more (= *mehr*) time.

Unit 4 – Time and date

2 – _Shall we_ buy her some flowers?

– _Yes, that's a good idea_. _Let's_ buy roses. She likes roses.

– _Shall we_ buy them this evening? There's a flower shop near my office.

3 – _Let's_ go to the restaurant in Linton Road. _We can_ have a pizza there.

– Oh no, not pizza again. _Shall we_ go to the Beehive _instead_?

They have got very good hamburgers there.

4 – _Shall we_ go to the London Transport Museum this afternoon?

– _Well, I'm not really interested in_ old cars, buses and trains. _Let's_ go to Madame Tussaud's _instead_.

5 Wie man das englische Datum schreibt und sagt

5th January, 1988 — the fifth of January, nineteen eighty-eight

5 April, 1986 — the fifth of April, nineteen eighty-six

	We write	We say
15/9/1941	_15th September, 1941_	_the fifteenth of September nineteen forty one_
23/11/1977	_23th November, 1977_	_the twenty third of November nineteen seventy seven_

25

Unit 4 – Time and date

1/3/1961 _____ _____
_____

22/2/1993 _____ _____
_____

16/8/1854 _____ _____
_____

2/6/1999 _____ _____
_____

6 (a) Wie man fragt, ob jemand etwas hat, und wie man auf solche Fragen antwortet

> – Have you/they got . . . ?   – Yes. I/we/they have.
>   No, I/we/they haven't.
>
> have got = haben

Fragen Sie die Verkäufer/innen des Kaufhauses, ob sie folgende Artikel haben, und vervollständigen Sie die Antworten.

1 – _Have you got_ Kodak films?

– I'm sorry, we _haven't_ Kodak films, but _we have got_ Ilford films.

2 – _Have you got_ a brown T-shirt in size 42?

– I'm sorry, _I haven't_ a brown T-shirt in your size,

but _I have_ a nice red T-shirt.

3 – _Have you got_ Commodore home computers?

– Well, _I have_ Commodore computers, but _I have got_ only

_____ the Commodore 2000.

4 – _____ a good camera for £150?

– Well, _____ one for £165; it's a very good camera from Japan.

(b) Wie man sagt, was jemand hat/nicht hat

> They've got . . . ./They haven't got.

Fassen Sie zusammen, was das Kaufhaus hat/nicht hat.

They '_____ Ilford films, but they _____ Kodak films. _____ a brown T-shirt in the right size, but _____ a red T-shirt. _____ Commodore home computers, but _____ only _____ the Commodore 2000. _____ a camera from Japan for £165.

7 Wie man sagt, was jemand hat/nicht hat

	have got		haven't got
I you we they		I you we they	
he she		**has got**	two children / three children

Fill in **have(n't)/has(n't) got**.

1 Hilltown _has got_ three small shops, but it _hasn't got_ a supermarket.

2 The Sunhill is a very good hotel. They _have got_ nice rooms, but they _haven't_ got TV in the rooms.

3 – Shall we buy this shirt for Mary?
– Oh no, she _has got_ already _____ three red shirts.

4 We _have got_ some jazz records, but we _haven't got_ a Louis Armstrong record.

5 Bob _has got_ a new German camera. It's a very good one, but quite expensive.

6 They _have got_ a nice house (= *Haus*) in the city, but they _haven't got_ a garden.

Unit 4 – Time and date

8 Wie man ausdrückt, für wen etwas bestimmt ist

I	you	he	she	we	they
▼	▼	▼	▼	▼	▼
for **me**	for **you**	for **him**	for **her**	for **us**	for **them**

*Fill in **I**, **me**, ...*

John Redman is back (= *zurück*)
from a business (= *Geschäfts-*) trip.
He has got a lot of presents in his suitcase.

John – Where's Lucy? I've got an umbrella for ___her___ ¹.

– And where's Roger? I've got a record for ___him___ ².

– Pam, I've got a blouse for ___you___ ³.

– And this is a Bach record for ___us___ ⁴. (= you + me)

– And these are for the Greens. I've got some Irish stamps for ___them___ ⁵.

Pam – Lucy, Dad has got an umbrella for ___you___ ⁶.

– Roger, Dad has got a record for ___you___ ⁷.

– Brian and Alan, Dad has got posters for ___you___ ⁸.

– Oh, John, what a nice blouse! Is it for ___me___ ⁹?

– John, I've got a present for ___you___ ¹⁰, too.

9 Time and date

In den Buchstaben sind 12 Wörter und 2 Abkürzungen versteckt, die zu den obengenannten Wortfeldern passen. Streichen Sie die gefundenen Wörter durch.

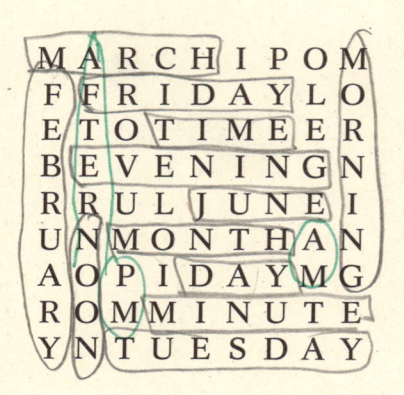

```
M A R C H I P O M
F F R I D A Y L O
E T O T I M E E R
B E V E N I N G N
R R U L J U N E I
U N M O N T H A N
A O P I D A Y M G
R O M M I N U T E
Y N T U E S D A Y
```

10 London Transport Guided Tours

In association with ▶▶ **NATIONAL TRAVEL**

MORNING TOURS

NEW **London Views & Luncheon Cruise.**

Starting from Victoria Coach Station at 10.30. Finishing at Westminster Pier at about 14.45. Sundays, 25 May-7 September.
Includes boat fare and meal: £10.90 (under 14s £9.90).

Westminster & Changing the Guard.

Start from Victoria Coach Station at 10.00, back about 13.00.
Mondays to Saturdays, 29 March-24 October.
£5.00 (under 14s £3.70).

Unit 4 – Time and date

AFTERNOON TOURS
City & Tower.

Starting from Victoria Coach Station at 1400, back about 1715.
Mondays to Saturdays, 29 March-24 October.
Sundays, 25 May-7 September.
Includes all admission charges: £6.70 (under 14s £4.60).

Madame Tussaud's & Museum of London.

Starting from Victoria Coach Station at 1400, back about 1715.
Wednesdays, 28 May-24 September.
Includes all admission charges: £6.00 (under 14s £4.00).

DAY TOURS
Canterbury & Dover.

Starting from Victoria Coach Station at 0830, back at about 1800.
Fridays, 9 May-26 September.
Includes lunch and all admission charges: £13.60 (under 14s £11.00).

IN TOWN
London Day Tour.

Starting from Victoria Coach Station at 1000, back about 1715.
Mondays to Saturdays, 29 March-24 October.
Includes lunch and all admission charges: £12.70 (under 14s £9.40).

EVENING TOURS
River Thames Cruise.

Starting from Victoria Coach Station at 1900, back about 2200.
Thursdays, 29 May-25 September.
Includes boat fare and buffet meal: £10.90.

Night Sights. *(Anblick)* — NEW

Starting from Victoria Coach Station at 1900.
Wednesdays, 28 May-24 September.
Includes meal and evening spectacular: £12.50.

---

1. You are in London on 28th May, but it is a business (= *Geschäfts-*) trip. You can see London only in the evening.

   Name of the tour: _Night Sights_
   It starts at: _Victoria Coach Station at 19.00_
   It costs (= *kostet*): _£12.50_

2. You are in London on 7th September. You haven't got time in the morning, and you want to meet friends at 6 p.m.

   Name of the tour: _City & Tower_
   It starts at: _Victoria Coach Station at 14.00_
   It costs: _£6.70_

3. You are in London on 30th March. You've only got time in the morning. Is there a cheap (= *billig*) tour (£5 or £6) for you?

   Name of the tour: _Westminster & Changing the guard_
   It starts at: ____
   It costs: ____

4. You are in London on 9th May. You'd like to start the tour after 9 a.m.

   Name of the tour: _In town, London day tour_
   It starts at: ____
   It costs: ____

Unit 4 – Time and date

11 *Vervollständigen Sie den Briefausschnitt.*
1 Sagen Sie, was Sie davon halten, daß Cathy mit dem Zug kommt.
2 Fragen Sie, ob Sie Cathy am Bahnhof treffen sollen.
3 Schlagen Sie vor, mit ihr essen zu gehen.

Dear Cathy,
I think <u>it's a good idea</u> <u>of you</u> to <u>go</u> by train. <u>Shall we meet</u> at <u>the station</u>? <u>We can go</u> to Flanagan's and have dinner* before we go home.
…

* eine Mahlzeit einnehmen

Unit 5 Invitations

I would like you to ~~come~~ come...
I would like to invite you to my

1 Wie man jemanden einlädt

> Would you like to + **verb** ... ?

Ask your friend

1 to come to your birthday party.
   _____ my _____?

2 to go to the cinema with you.
   _____ me _____?

3 to see your garden.
   _____ our _____?

4 to listen to your Bob Dylan records.
   _____?

5 to go to a pub with you and your friend.
   _____ me my _____?

2 Wie man etwas ausdrückt, was gerade oder in naher Zukunft geschieht

| I | **am** | working | (a) **at the moment** (= *zur Zeit, gerade*). |
| you/we | **are** | | (b) **tonight/tomorrow/**... (= *nahe Zukunft*). |

*Fill in the right form of the **Present Progressive** (= Verlaufsform in der Gegenwart).*

1 – We _are having_ (have) a party on Saturday.
   Are you _coming_ (come), too?

2 – I _'m going_ (go) to Florida next week.
   Where _are_ you _going_ (go) this year, to Canada again?

3 – What _are_ you _doing_ (do) at the bank?
   – I _'m changing_ (change) money. I _'m going_ (go) to Germany next week.

4 – Ah, you _are working_ (work) in the garden again?
   – Yes, we _are going_ (go) on a trip at the weekend.

5 – We _are selling_ (sell) our car because
   we _are buying_ (buy) another one next month.

Unit 5 – Invitations

3 Wie man die Ablehnung einer Einladung begründet

These people cannot come to a party. Write down why they cannot come.

1 *Jill hat auch eine Party.*

Jill: – I'm sorry, but ___I'm having a party___, too.

2 *Cathy und Alex gehen in ein Konzert.*

Cathy and Alex: – ___That's a pity___, but ___we are going in a concert___.

3 *John trifft einen Freund.*

John: – I'm afraid I can't come. ___I'm meeting a friend___.

4 *Jennifer arbeitet heute abend.*

Jennifer: – ___I'm___ sorry, but ___I'm working___ tonight.

5 *Die Tompsons haben Gäste.*

Mr and Mrs Tompson: – ___We are___ sorry, but ___we are having guests___.

4 Wie man Einladungen oder Bitten um Hilfe einleiten, und wie man darauf antworten kann

> – What are you doing at the moment/on .../next ...?
>   – (a) I'm ... ing ....
>   (b) Oh, nothing, really.
> – (a) Oh, I'm ... ing .... It's a pity you can't come.
>   (b) Oh, good. Could you perhaps help/...?

Vervollständigen Sie die Dialoge.

1 *Janet arbeitet im Garten. Sie möchte, daß Fred ihr hilft. Fred tut nichts Besonderes.*

Janet: – Fred, ___what are you doing___ at the moment?

Fred: – ___Oh, nothing, really___.

Janet: – I'm ___working in the garden. Would you like to help___ me?

2 *Angela möchte Freitagabend ins Kino gehen und sucht deshalb einen Babysitter. Sie fragt ihre Nachbarn. Ihre Nachbarn haben nichts vor.*

Angela: – ___What are you doing___ on Friday evening?

Unit 5 – Invitations

Neighbours: – _Oh nothing really_.

Angela: – I'd like to _go to the cinema_.
Would you like to look after the baby?

3 *Roy möchte Janice zu seiner Geburtstagsparty am nächsten Samstag einladen. Janice geht nächsten Freitag in Urlaub.*

Roy: – What _are you doing_ next _Saturday_ ?

Janice: – _Oh, I'm going_ on holiday _next Friday_.

Roy: – Oh, _I'm having_ my birthday party on _Saturday_.
It's a pity you can't come.

5 Wie man fragt, ob jemand etwas gerade/in naher Zukunft macht, und wie man auf solche Fragen antwortet

Mrs Grey is at home after a conference. She would like to know (= *wissen*) what the family is doing.

Complete (= vervollständigen Sie) Mrs Grey's questions and Mr Grey's answers.

Mrs Grey – _____ Paul _____ (do) his homework?

Mr Grey – No, _____ _____. _____ _____ (phone) a friend.

Mrs Grey – Hm. _____ Grandpa (= *Großvater*) _____ (watch) TV?

Mr Grey – Yes, _____ _____. He _____ _____ (sit) in his room.

Mrs Grey – _____ Ann and Andrew _____ (play) with their computer?

Mr Grey – Yes, _____ _____. And they _____ _____ (listen) to records.

Mrs Grey – _____ you _____ (go) to night school tonight?

Mr Grey – No, I' _____ not.

Mrs Grey – _____ we _____ (have) dinner now?

Mr Grey – No, we _____. We _____ _____ (have) pizza at Gino's.

Unit 5 – Invitations

6 Wie man beschreibt, was Leute gerade machen

It is 9 p.m. Write down what the people are doing.

Third floor:

Mrs Grey ___is___ ___helping___ ___her___ son with ___his___ homework, and her daughter ___is___ ___washing___ ___her___ hair.

Second floor:

Mr and Mrs Smith ___are___ ___listening___ ___to___ records and ___their___ children ___are___ ___playing___.

First floor:

The Johnsons ___are___ ___having___ a party and ___their___ daughter ___is___ ___reading___ comics.

Ground floor:

Cindy ___is___ ___writing___ letters and Roy and Tom ___are___ ___looking___ ___a___ video film.

34

7 Wie man Aussage- und Fragesätze im **Present Progressive** bildet

What are they doing at the moment?

Write sentences in the Present Progressive.

1 Peter – take – a picture of Susan
_____.

2 The tourists – listen to – the guide
_____.

3 John and Sue – play – tennis
_____.

4 You – learn – English
_____.

5 They – watch – an interesting video
_____.

And now make questions from sentences 1, 3, 4.

1 Is Peter taking _____?
3 _____?
4 _____?

8 Wie man -ing-Formen von Verben schreibt

*Fill in the **-ing forms** of these verbs: change, leave, invite, phone, plan, sit, talk, take, write*

1 TALKING
2 TAKING
3 SITTING
4 WRITING
5 LEAVING
6 CHANGING
7 INVITING
8 PLANNING
9 PHONING

Unit 5 – Invitations

9 Wortschatzrätsel zu den Wörtern aus Unit 5

1 *Guest* – I'd like a glass of French ... .

2 – You can't ... him to your party, he's on holiday in Canada.

3 – You need a ... when you want to go to the theatre.

4 – The bus is already five minutes ... .

5 – 60 minutes are one ... .

6 – Sheila gets a lot of ... from her friend in America.

7 – We like going on holiday in ... .

8 – Would you like to see the ... of my holidays in Canada?

9 – Cliff is watching TV ... he is having his dinner.

10 – I can't take good pictures with this old camera. I need a ... camera.

11 – I like being with other people, I like being in a ... .

12 – There is a very ... film on TV today.

Crossword answers:
1. WINE
2. INVITE
3. TICKET
4. LATE
5. HOUR
6. LETTERS
7. SUMMER
8. PICTURES
9. WHILE
10. NEW
11. GROUP

10

> Dear Janet,
>   It's my birthday next Friday and I'm having a party on Saturday. Can you and Fred come? Please let me know by Sunday if you can come.
>   Yours, Cindy

Schreiben Sie einen Antwortbrief zu folgenden Stichpunkten:

Dank für die Einladung – können leider nicht kommen – fahren am Montag in Urlaub nach Italien

_____

_____
_____
_____
_____

Stop Over Test 1 (zu bearbeiten nach Unit 5)

Zur Arbeitsweise:

1 Versuchen Sie, die Testaufgaben zu lösen.
2 Überprüfen Sie Ihre Lösungen anhand des Schlüssels im Anhang des Arbeitsbuchs.
3 Wenn Sie Fehler gemacht haben,
   • schlagen Sie in dem Abschnitt in der Grammatikübersicht des Lehrbuchs nach, auf den verwiesen wird,
   • versuchen Sie dann noch einmal, die Aufgabe zu lösen.

1 *Fill in the right **pronouns** (= Fürwörter).*

Peter — Hello, Frank?

Frank — Hello, how are __you__ [1]?

Peter — __I__ [2]'m fine, thank you. And __you__ [3]?

Frank — Very well, thanks. This is Jane. She works in __our__ [4] office. Jane, this is Peter Banks and this is __his__ [5] wife Helen. Peter and Helen are from Brighton. __They__ [6] have got a nice house there. __Their__ [7] daughter works for Green & Son.

Helen — How do __you__ [8] do?

Jane — How do __you__ [9] do?

Frank — Shall __we__ [10] all (= alle) go to Gino's? __We__ [11] can have pizza there.

Helen — That's a good idea. Peter and __I__ [12] like pizza.

Peter and Helen — But __we__ [13] have to phone __our__ [14] daughter first. __She__ [15] is at home now and ...

Siehe Grammatikübersicht G 1(a), (b)

2 *Fill in the right **personal pronouns**.*

a — Can you help
__me__ [1] (mir)?
__them__ [2] (ihnen)?
__us__ [3] (uns)?
__him__ [4] (ihm)?
__her__ [5] (ihr)?

b — Is this for
__you__ [1] (dich)?
__her__ [2] (sie = Helen)?
__him__ [3] (ihn)?
__you__ [4] (euch) two?
__you__ [5] (Sie), Mr White?

Siehe Grammatikübersicht G 1(a)

Stop Over – Test 1

3 *Fill in this, that, these or those.*

1 – Is ___this___ a postcard from Italy?
– No, it isn't. It's from Germany. The one over there, ___that___'s a postcard from Italy.

2 – Are ___those___ your keys, the keys near the telephone over there?

3 Cliff – ___This___ is my wife. Alison, ___this___ is Mr Parks. He is my German teacher.
Alison – How do you do.
Mr Parks – How do you do.

4 – Oh no, not the ones over there. Look here, ___these___ flowers are nice,
– I'd like some of ___these___, please.

Siehe Grammatikübersicht G 1(d)

4 *Fill in the right question words (= Fragewörter).*

1 – That's Roger McGregor.
– ___Who___ is it?
– Roger McGregor.

2 – My name's Fulton.
– ___What___'s your name?
– Fulton.

3 – ___How much___ much is it?
– It's three pounds.

4 – ___What time___ is the next bus to Buxton?
– At six o'clock.

5 – ___Where___ is Eric?
– He's in the garden.

6 – Directory Inquiries. ___Which___ town, please?

7 – This is Tracey's car.
– ___Whose___ car?
– Tracey Green's car.

Siehe Grammatikübersicht G 1(c)

5 **A or an?**

1 ___an___ Irish pub
2 ___an___ office
3 ___an___ English book
4 ___an___ umbrella

5 ___a___ newspaper
6 ___an___ American restaurant
7 ___a___ shop assistant
8 ___an___ assistant

Siehe Grammatikübersicht G 2

6 **Singular (= Einzahl) or plural (= Mehrzahl)?**

– I live in an old ___house___¹ (house) in a ___village___² (village), twenty ___minutes___³ (minute) from the ___city___⁴ (city). I've got three ___children___⁵ (child), all (= alle) ___girls___⁶ (girl). Sheila is only seven ___months___⁷ (month) old. My ___husband___⁸ (husband) works in an ___office___⁹ (office) in the city.

He comes home very late and he hasn't got much time to play with the ___children___¹⁰ (child).

Stop Over – Test 1

I only buy small ___things___ ¹¹ (thing) in the village. For ___shoes___ ¹² (shoe), ___dress___ ¹³ (dress) or ___blouses___ ¹⁴ (blouse) I go to one of the three department ___stores___ ¹⁵ (store) in the city. A lot of other ___housewives___ ¹⁶ (housewife) in the village go shopping in the city, too. . . .

Siehe Grammatikübersicht G 3(a)

7 –'s–genitive or genitive with of?

Wem oder wozu gehören diese Dinge?

1 ___Mr Smith's garden___ (Mr Smith – garden) is very nice.
2 What's ___the colour of your car___ (the colour – your car)?
3 The ___guest's nationality___ (nationality – guest) is German.
4 ___men's shoes___ (men – shoes) are on the third floor.
5 Can you tell me ___the size of that blouse___ (that blouse – the size)?
6 ___girls' pullovers___ (pullovers – girls) are over there.
7 The ___address of the cinema___ (address – the cinema) is 18 Church Road.
8 The ___number of that building___ (that building – number) is 17.

Siehe Grammatikübersicht G 3(b)

8 *Fill in the right forms of* **be**.

– Where ___are___ ¹ you from?
– I'___m___ ² from Edinburgh and my wife ___is___ ³ from Glasgow but we live in London now.
  I'___m___ ⁴ an engineer and there ___isn't___ ⁵ n't much work for engineers in Scotland.
– ___Are___ ⁶ your children in London, too?
– No, they ___aren't___ ⁷ n't. They ___are___ ⁸ still in Scotland. Margaret ___is___ ⁹ a secretary and Fred ___is___ ¹⁰ a waiter. ___Are___ ¹¹ you and your wife from Scotland, too?
– We ___are___ ¹² from London. My husband works in a factory and I'___m___ ¹³ a housewife. Our daughter ___is___ ¹⁴ a waitress.

Siehe Grammatikübersicht G 6.1(a)

9 *Fill in the right forms of* **have got**. *Use the* **long forms**.

1 Jane ___has got___ three white skirts but she ___hasn't got___ a red one.
2 We ___have got___ two cars but we ___haven't got___ a garage.
3 Excuse me, ___have___ you ___got___ the time, please?

39

Stop Over – Test 1

4 The Taylors __have got__ four children, they are all girls.

5 What __has__ he __got__ there? Is it a telephone directory?

10 *Write down the short forms for the long forms of* **have (not) got**.

1 I have got = __I've got__

2 I have not got = __I haven't got__

3 He has got = __He's got__

4 She has not got = __She hasn't got__

5 They have got = __They've got__

Siehe Grammatikübersicht G 6.1(b)

11 *Fill in the right forms (= Formen) of the* **present progressive** *(= Verlaufsform der Gegenwart).*

– Hello, Fred. This __is__ Peter Brown __speaking__ (speak).

– Hello, Peter. Where __are__ you __phoning__ (phone) from?

– I'__m phoning__ (phone) from my hotel room. I'm at the Garden Hotel.

– Is your wife with you?

– No, she isn't. She's at home with Johnny. He'__s going__ (go) to school next week. What __are__ you and Jane __doing__ (do) at the moment?

– We'__re watching__ (watch) TV.

– I'__m going__ (go) to the theatre tonight to see 'Evita'. Would you like to come with me?

– Just a moment, please. The children __are coming__ (come) in and I would like to . . . .

Siehe Grammatikübersicht G 6.3(d); zu den Kurzformen von **be** siehe auch G 6.1(a)

12 *Write short answers.*

1 – Can you do your shopping in England on Sunday? – __No__, __I can't__.

2 – Has Frankfurt got an airport? – __Yes__, __it has__.

3 – Is a Mercedes an expensive car? – __Yes__, __it is__.

4 – Is "Karstadt" a department store? – __Yes__, __it is__.

5 – Have the Americans got big cars? – __Yes__, __they have__.

6 – Can you buy directories in a department store? – __No__, __you can't__.

7 – Are shops open in Germany at 8 p.m.? – __No__, __they aren't__.

8 – Have you got a car? – __Yes__, __I have__.

Siehe Grammatikübersicht G 7(c)

13 Ordnen Sie die Wörter den richtigen **Wortfeldern** zu.

afternoon, airport, bank, cinema, department store, engineer, evening, factory, guide, hairdresser, holiday, hospital, hour, housewife, month, night, school, secretary, shop, shop assistant, station, teacher, tomorrow, tonight, waiter, waitress, week

Buildings	Jobs	Time
airport	engineer	afternoon
bank	guide	evening
cinema	hairdresser	holiday
department store	housewife	hour
factory	secretary	month
hospital	shop assistant	night
school	teacher	tomorrow
shop	waiter	tonight
station	waitress	week

addresses, ask, buy, coats, jeans, letters, magazines, names, newspapers, numbers, play, postcards, sell, shirts, shoes, skirts, socks, suits, take pictures, telephone directories, trousers, watch, work, write

What you can wear	What you can read	What you can do
coats	addresses	ask
jeans	letters	buy
shirts	magazines	play
shoes	names	sell
skirts	newspapers	take pictures
socks	numbers	watch
suits	postcards	work
trousers	telephone directories	write

14 *Entscheiden Sie, ob hinter Sätze, in denen diese **Redewendungen** vorkommen, ein Fragezeichen oder ein Punkt gehört.*

1 Are they... [?] 2 ..., isn't it [?] 3 Be careful [.] 4 Is that you [?] 5 Can they... [?]

6 Is there... [?] 7 Excuse me [.] 8 Let's... [.] 9 Goodbye [.] 10 Shall we... [?]

11 Have you got... [?] 12 See you [.] 13 Hello [.] 14 You're wrong [.]

15 How much is it [?] 16 Yes, speaking [.] 17 I'd like... [.] 18 What size [?]

19 I'm afraid... [.] 20 Would you like... [?]

Unit 6 Every day...

1 Wie ich sage, was ich regelmäßig tue

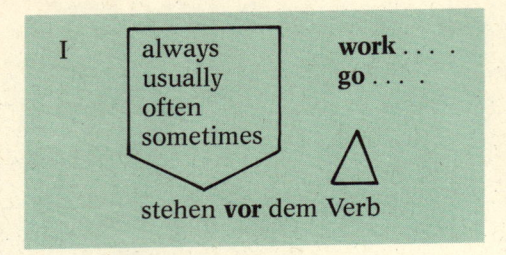

> I always / usually / often / sometimes   **work**.... **go**....
> stehen **vor** dem Verb

*Write down what you **usually, always, sometimes, often** do, and **when**.*

read the newspaper – phone friends – watch TV – go to the cinema – write a letter

1 *I usually read the newspaper in the morning.*
2 _____
3 _____
4 _____
5 _____

2 Wie man sagt, was jemand regelmäßig tut

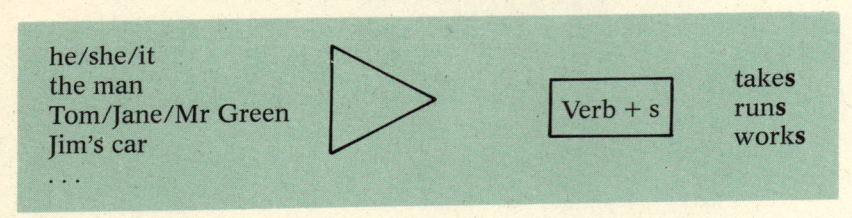

> he/she/it
> the man
> Tom/Jane/Mr Green
> Jim's car
> ...
> Verb + s
> takes / runs / work**s**

Look at the information about Angela White. Say how often she does things in the morning.

	always	usually	often	sometimes
1 listen to the radio				x
2 go to the bathroom	x			
3 have a shower		x		
4 have breakfast before 7.30		x		
5 read the morning paper			x	
6 start work at 8 o'clock		x		
7 make a cup of tea in the office			x	

Unit 6 – Every day...

1 She _____.
2 _____.
3 _____.
4 _____.
5 _____.
6 _____.
7 _____.

3 Wie man regelmäßig wiederkehrendes Geschehen, und wie man augenblickliches oder zukünftiges Geschehen beschreibt

> **present simple** (*einfache Gegenwart*)
> I often **go** to the cinema.
> They sometimes **phone** their mother.   } *regelmäßig wiederkehrendes Geschehen*
> We usually **leave** the house at seven o'clock.
>
> **present progressive**
> – Where's Alice?
>   – She**'s working** (*zur Zeit, gerade*) in the garden.
> – I**'m going** to the theatre tonight (*nahe Zukunft*).

*Fill in **present simple** or **present progressive**.*

1 – Would you like to come to the pub with me?

   – I'm sorry, but I _____ (work/ 'm working) in the garden.

2 – I usually _____ (am playing/play) tennis at this time of the evening but tonight

   I _____ (go/ 'm going) to the cinema.

3 – The Whites often _____ (go/are going) to concerts with us, but tonight they

   aren't _____ (go/going) because they _____ (are having/have)

   a party.

4 – Where are Rose and Mary?

   – They are in the bathroom. They _____ (wash/ are washing) their hair.

5 – What are your children doing?

   – I think they _____ (are watching/watch) TV.

   – Why?

   – Because they usually _____ (are watching/watch) TV in the evening.

Unit 6 – Every day . . .

4 Wie man Fragen mit **Hilfsverben** stellt

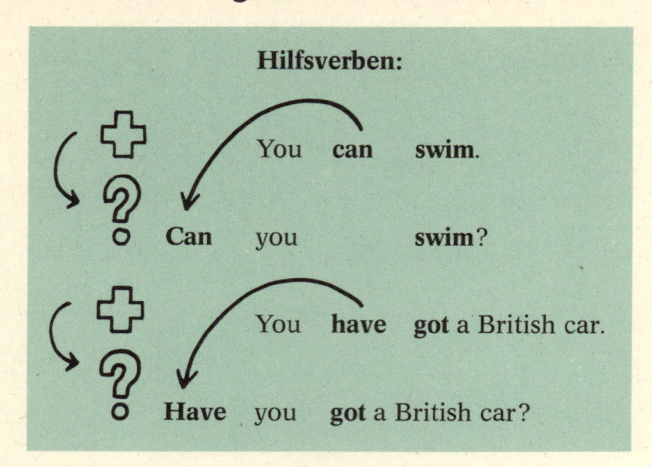

Hilfsverben:

You **can** swim.
Can you swim?

You **have** got a British car.
Have you got a British car?

Ask your teacher if he/she

1 is from England.
2 has got a lot of English books.
3 can speak German.
4 he/she is good at sports.

1 _____?
2 _____?
3 _____?
4 _____?

5 Wie man Fragen mit **Do + Vollverb** stellt

Vollverben:

You speak English.
Do you speak English?

Ask your teacher if he/she

1 speaks British or American English.
2 likes American cars.
3 wants to go on holiday to England.
4 sometimes goes to see English films.
5 often reads English books.
6 drives a foreign car.

1 *Do you speak* _____?
2 _____?
3 _____?
4 _____?
5 _____?
6 _____?

6 Wie man auf **Ja/Nein-Fragen** antwortet

Ordnen Sie die Kurzantworten den Fragen zu.

– **Do** you live in Brighton?   – Yes, I **do**.
                                  No, I **do**n't.
– **Have** you **got** a brother? – Yes, I **have**.
                                  No, I **have**n't.
– **Are** you from London?   – Yes, I **am**.
                                  No, I'm not.

1 – Do you learn English every day?
2 – Can you speak another foreign language?
3 – Have your children got American friends?
4 – Do your children go to school?
5 – Are your friends in the garden?
6 – Can Tom and Eric help me with my computer?
7 – Has your English teacher got an English car?

a – Yes, they do.   d – Yes, they are.   g – Yes, he/she has / – No, he/she hasn't.
b – No, they can't.   e – No, I don't.
c – No, I can't.   f – No, they haven't.

1 _____ 2 _____ 3 _____ 4 _____ 5 _____ 6 _____ 7 _____

7 Wie man Fragen mit **do, does** stellt und darauf antwortet

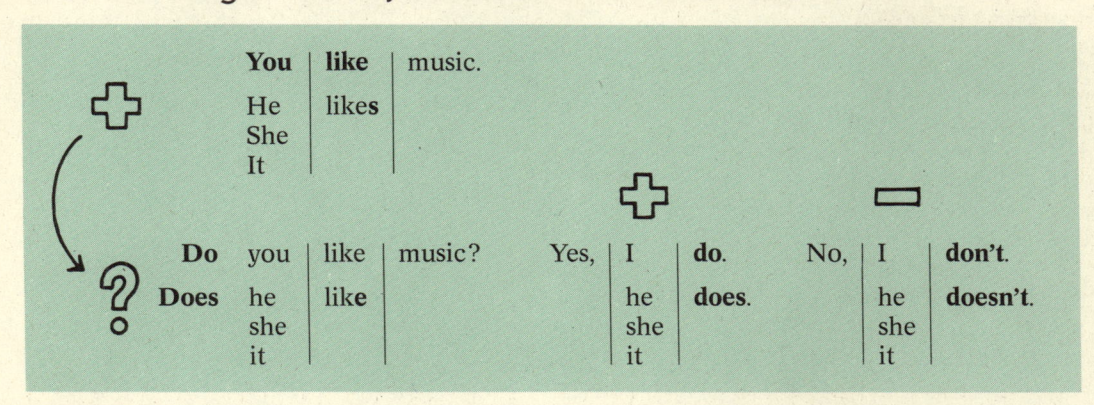

	You / He / She / It	like / likes	music.

| ? | Do you / Does he / she / it | like | music? | Yes, I / he / she / it | do. / does. | No, I / he / she / it | don't. / doesn't. |

John, Paul and Jennifer work for National Express in London. They do not work on Saturdays. Jennifer speaks two foreign languages (French and German). John and Paul only speak English. They all like working with people. John and Jennifer live in Boreham Wood and Paul lives in Croydon. John drives an English car and Jennifer and Paul drive German cars.

*Fill in **do/does** and **the right verbs** in the questions and write down the answers.*

1 – _____ John and Jennifer _____ in Croydon?
   – _____.

2 – _____ they _____ on Saturdays?
   – _____.

3 – _____ Jennifer _____ German?
   – _____.

4 – _____ John and Paul _____ a foreign language?
   – _____.

5 – _____ John, Paul and Jennifer _____ working with people?
   – _____.

6 – _____ Paul _____ in Croydon?
   – _____.

7 – _____ Jennifer _____ in Croydon, too?
   – _____.

8 – _____ John _____ an English car?
   – _____.

9 – _____ Paul and Jennifer _____ French cars?
   – _____.

Unit 6 – Every day...

8 Wie man Fragen mit einleitenden Fragewörtern stellt

Job interview

Cathy is a waitress and her husband Roger is a taxi driver.

You want to know from **Cathy**

1 *where she works.*
2 *how she travels to work.*
3 *when Roger usually starts work.*
4 *what their children do when they are at work.*
5 *when Roger usually gets home.*
6 *how often they have dinner with their children.*
7 *what she thinks about her job.*

	I	**like**	fast cars.
	Jim Claire	likes	
What	**do** does	you he she	lik**e**?

Now ask Cathy.

1 - _____?
2 - _____?
3 - _____?
4 - _____?
5 - _____?
6 - _____?
7 - _____?

9 Wie man Vollverben verneint

＋	−
I/you/we/they **like**	I/you/we/they **don't like** ....
He/she/(it) speak**s**	He/she/(it) **doesn't** speak ....

*Ergänzen Sie, was diese Leute **nicht machen/nicht mögen**.*

1 - I often work in the evenings, but _____ on Sundays.

2 - Penny likes her work, but _____ her boss.

3 - I think Eric can help you with your car, but _____ he can help you today.

4 - They get up very early every day, but _____ before 10 a.m. on Sundays.

5 - We sometimes work in the garden, but _____ usually _____ there very long.

6 - I know Roger, but _____ his wife.

Unit 6 – Every day...

10 Wie man Bedauern und Mitgefühl ausdrückt oder, daß man sich mit jemandem freut

Bedauern/Mitgefühl
– Oh, how terrible!
– Oh, dear!
– I'm sorry to hear that.

Freude/Mitfreude
– Oh, good.
– I'm glad to hear that!
– Oh, how nice for you!
– Congratulations!

Write down what you would say to these persons.

1 – I've got a new car. It's the red one over there.
   – _____

2 – Jack has to go to hospital next month.
   – _____

3 – Donna is feeling fine today.
   – _____

4 – I'm going on holiday to Italy next week.
   – _____

5 – I can't find my new camera.
   – _____

11 *Streichen Sie aus jeder Reihe ein Wort durch, das nicht zu den anderen paßt.*

1 often – always – usually – every
2 once – first – three times – twice
3 news – shower – bathroom – to wash
4 among – between – all – at
5 underground – passenger – bus – car
6 to leave – to agree – to arrive – to get back
7 interesting – terrible – every – unpleasant
8 early – more – late – at night
9 to feel – to hear – to forget – to see

Schlagen Sie die Wörter, deren Bedeutung Sie vergessen haben, im Vokabelverzeichnis der Unit oder im alphabetischen Vokabelverzeichnis nach.

Unit 6 – Every day ...

12 *Dieser Briefausschnitt wird Ihnen vorgelesen. Sie können die unterstrichenen Wörter nicht verstehen; fragen Sie danach.*

> You ask me about my private life but I'm afraid there isn't much to tell! I go <u>to a Folk Song Club</u>¹ every week and I also learn <u>Spanish</u>² at night school in the evening. The other evenings I just sit in the <u>living-room</u>³, read the <u>newspaper</u>⁴ or watch TV. Oh yes, I sometimes play the <u>guitar</u>⁵; it's a birthday present from Peter. What about you?

1 <u>Where does she go every week</u> ?
2 _____ ?
3 _____ ?
4 _____ ?
5 _____ ?

Write down the **full verbs (= Vollverben)** in this letter.

a _____   b _____   c _____   d _____
e _____   f _____   g _____   h _____

*Schreiben Sie einen ähnlichen Briefausschnitt über eine/n Bekannte/n, in dem Sie deren/dessen Freizeitaktivitäten und Hobbies schildern. Beachten Sie dabei die **s-Endung** bei den **Verben**, wenn Sie über Ihre/n Bekannte/n schreiben.*

Unit 7 Travelling in Britain

1 Wie man Vorlieben begründet

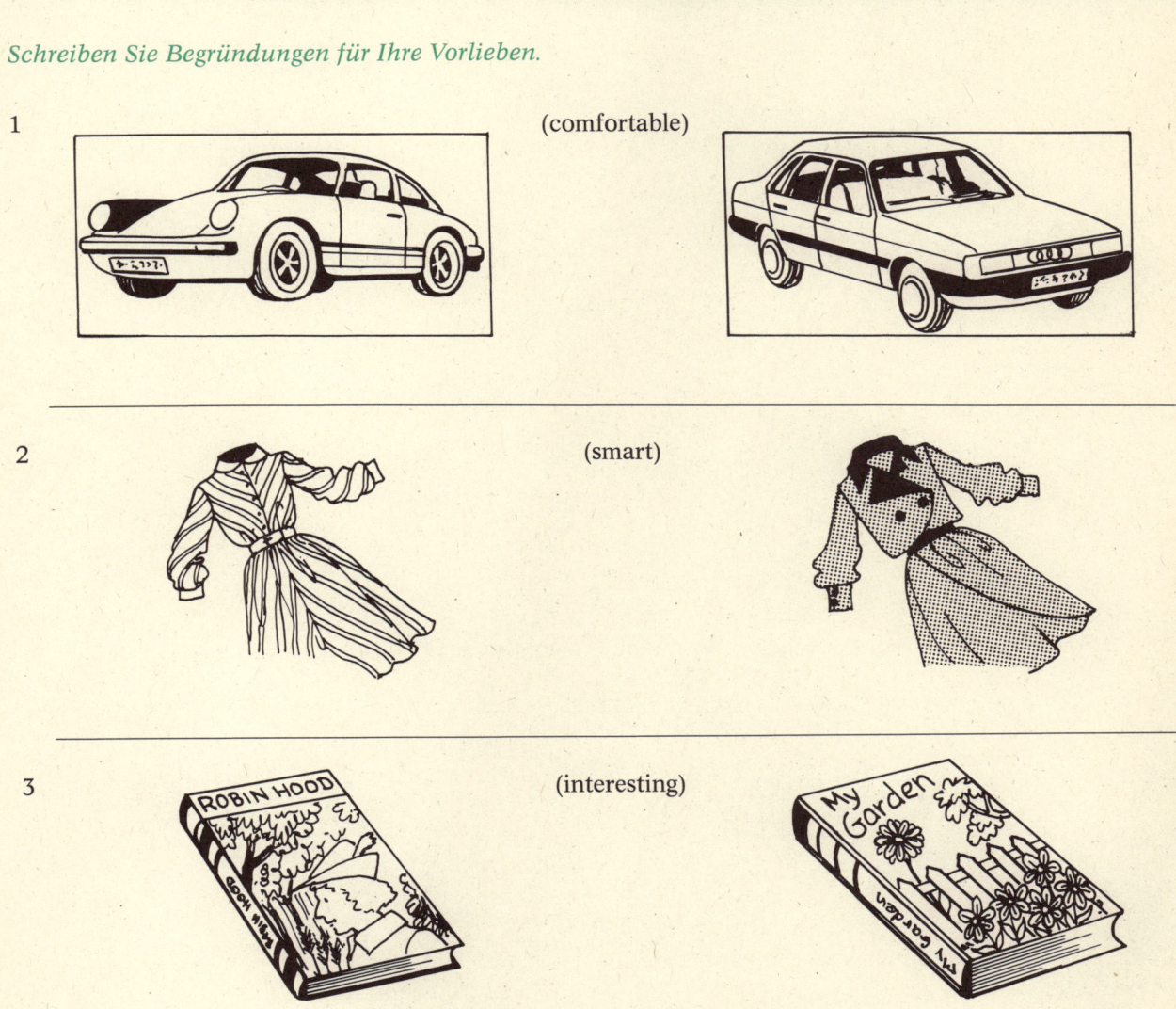

(cheap)

I prefer the coat on the left because it is cheaper.

Steigerung

short words: cheap, cheap**er** [**!** big, bi**gg**er]
long words: interesting, **more** interesting

Schreiben Sie Begründungen für Ihre Vorlieben.

1 (comfortable)

2 (smart)

3 (interesting)

49

Unit 7 – Travelling in Britain

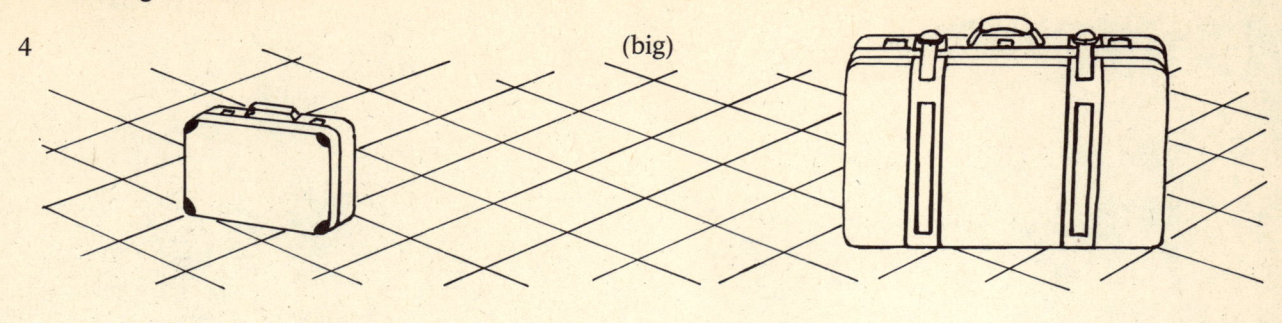

4   (big)

_____

2   Wie man Ratschläge gibt

> – I'd . . . , because . . . .
>
> – You should . . . .
>
> – I think it's . . . er/more . . . to . . . .

Geben Sie Ratschläge.

1 – I can go by train, or I can go by car.

   Sie glauben, daß es mit dem Zug schneller geht.

   – _____.

2 – This pullover is too small.

   Sie schlagen vor, einen größeren Pullover zu kaufen.

   – _____?

3 – There's "Superman" at the Odeon and a film with Robert Redford at the Empire.

   Sie würden in den Film mit Robert Redford gehen, weil er interessanter ist.

   – _____
      _____.

4 – This car is terrible. There's always something wrong with it.

   Sie raten, ein anderes Auto zu kaufen.

   – _____?

Unit 7 – Travelling in Britain

3 Wie man Vergleiche anstellt

(just) as ... as (bei Gleichem)
... er/more ... than (bei Ungleichem)

1st

$245,000, 5 bedrooms, 2 bathrooms, 1982

2nd

$87,000, 3 bedrooms, 2 bathrooms, 1972

3rd

$87,000, 2 bedrooms, 1 bathroom, 1982

Compare:

1 the first and the second house – comfortable
_____.

2 the second and the third house – expensive
_____.

3 the first and the third house – big
_____.

4 the second and the third house – old
_____.

5 the garden of the first house and the garden of the third house – big
_____.

6 the first and the third house – old
_____.

51

Unit 7 – Travelling in Britain

4 Wie man Widerspruch ausdrückt

> – I think a Kadett is more comfortable than a Golf.
> – I'm afraid I don't agree. I think a Golf is | more comfortable than | a Kadett.
> | just as comfortable as |

Widersprechen Sie und berichtigen Sie die Aussagen.

1 – I think cars in America are more modern than cars in Germany.

   – _____
     _____.

2 – I think the Spar Market is more convenient than the Minimarket.

   – _____
     _____.

3 – I think that holidays in Germany are more expensive than holidays in England.

   – _____
     _____.

4 – I prefer to travel by train. I think it's safer than by plane.

   – _____
     _____.

5 Wie man Eigenschaftswörter steigert

Sie möchten wissen,

1 *welches das beste Auto ist.*
2 *wo der billigste Supermarkt ist.*
3 *wo das bequemste Restaurant ist.*
4 *wieviel die teuersten Schuhe kosten.*
5 *wer der netteste Verkäufer ist.*
6 *welches der interessanteste Film ist.*
7 *was das größte Gebäude ist.*

> short words: fast – faster – fast**est**
> long words: interesting – more interesting – **most** interesting
> Sonderfall: good – better – **best**

Ask the questions.

1 – Which _____?
2 – _____?
3 – _____?
4 – _____?
5 – _____?
6 – _____?
7 – _____?

Unit 7 – Travelling in Britain

6 Adjectives (= Eigenschaftswörter)

1. I haven't got much money (= *Geld*), so I always buy ... shoes.
2. This hotel is near the station, it's very ... for tourists.
3. Jane Fonda is a ... film star.
4. I have never got much time, so I need a ... car.
5. Vanessa speaks two ... languages.
6. A lot of tourists go to Brighton. It's a very ... place.
7. He doesn't talk very much, he's a very ... person.
8. You cannot open it with a normal key, you need a ... one.
9. I don't like him. I think he is ... .
10. He often drives too fast, he is not very ... .
11. I can listen to his stories for hours (= *stundenlang*), they are always very ... .
12. The Hilton is a very ... hotel, but it is quite expensive, too.

7 Garden House Hotel

Hans Schmidt und seine Frau wollen mit ihrer Tochter, ihrem Mann und deren Kind Maria (6) vom 16. – 19. August im Garden House Hotel übernachten.
Die Schmidts wohnen in 6000 Frankfurt, Karlstr. 5; ihre Telefonnummer ist 069/23794. Herr und Frau Schmidt möchten in einem Zimmer mit 2 Einzelbetten schlafen. Die Tochter und ihr Mann wollen mit ihrem Kind in einem Zimmer mit zwei Betten und Zusatzbett schlafen.

Können Sie das Buchungsformular für Hans Schmidt ausfüllen?

BOOKING FORM

Name _____

Address _____
_____
_____

Daytime Phone Number _____

Please reserve _____ (no. of) rooms

	Type of Room*)	No. of Adults	Name & Age of Children Sharing the Room
1st Room			
2nd Room			
3rd Room			

*) Type 'A' Room is with one double bed.
*) Type 'B' is with two beds.
*) Type 'C' is with two beds and a rollaway bed.

Date of arrival: _____ No. of nights: _____

Signed _____ Date _____

8

Schreiben Sie einen Briefausschnitt an eine/n englische/n Bekannte/n, in dem Sie zwei Hotels vergleichen. Der/Die Bekannte soll selbst entscheiden, wo er/sie wohnen will. Benutzen Sie bei den Vergleichen folgende Eigenschaftswörter: **quiet – comfortable – expensive**.

Parkhotel	near park	TV in every room	room with bath 100 DM
Wiesenhotel	2 minutes from the station	radio in every room	room with bath 100 DM

Unit 8 Food and drink

1 Wie man beim Frühstück
etwas bestellt

nach Wünschen fragen	bestellen
– Would you like . . . ?	– Can I have . . . , please?
– What would you like . . . ?	– . . . , please.

Vervollständigen Sie das Gespräch.

Waiter – Good morning, sir. _____[1] English[a] or Continental breakfast[b]?

Guest – English breakfast, _____[2].

Waiter – _____[3] some orange juice?

Guest – Yes, _____[4]. And _____[5] some cornflakes, _____?

Waiter – Yes, sir. And _____[6] then, sausages or bacon and eggs?

Guest – Bacon and eggs and toast, _____[7].

Waiter – _____[8] coffee or tea?

Guest – Tea, _____[9].

2 Wie man ein Essen bestellt

- I'd like . . . .
- I'll have/take . . . .
- Can I order/have . . . , please?

Fill in, please.

You: – Waiter! _____ the menu, _____?

Waiter: – Just a moment, madam/sir.

You: – _____ order now, _____?

Waiter: – Yes, madam/sir. What would you like to start with?

You: – _____ a tomato soup.

Waiter: – And what would you like to follow?

You: – _____.

Waiter: – Yes, madam/sir, steak with chips. And what would you like to drink?

You: – Well, I think _____ a glass of wine. What wine have you got?

Waiter: – We have got some very good French and German wines.

You: – _____ a glass of French red wine.

---

[a] **English breakfast** siehe Frühstückskarte auf S. 78 im Lehrbuch und S. 57 im Arbeitsbuch.
[b] **Continental breakfast** kleines Frühstück, bestehend aus Brot, Butter, Marmelade und Kaffee oder Tee.

Unit 8 – Food and drink

3 Wie man **some** benutzt

some (a) = „einige" ... (bei zählbaren Dingen)

(b) = „etwas" ... (bei **nicht** Zählbarem)

*Wird **some** in den folgenden Sätzen in der Bedeutung **(a)** oder **(b)** benutzt?*

1 There are some very good hotels in Wellington. _____
2 They have got some good wine. _____
3 There is some mineral water on the table. _____
4 I'll bring some pictures of my family along next week. _____
5 Would you like some ice in your coke? _____
6 There are some very expensive restaurants in Paris. _____
7 They have got some really good bacon at the Minimarket. _____

4 Wie man **any** und **some** benutzt

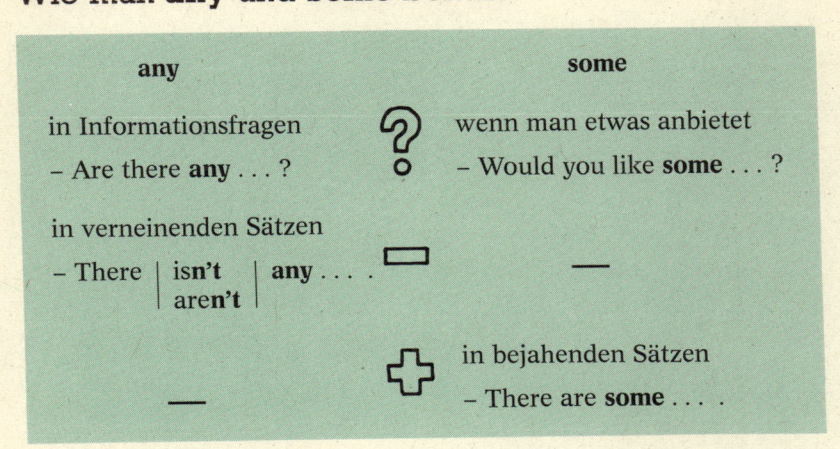

any

in Informationsfragen
– Are there **any** ... ?

in verneinenden Sätzen
– There isn't / aren't **any** ....

some

wenn man etwas anbietet
– Would you like **some** ... ?

in bejahenden Sätzen
– There are **some** ....

*Fill in **any** or **some**.*

1 – I'd like _____ tomato juice, please.

   – I'm sorry, we haven't got _____ tomato juice. Would you like _____ orange juice?

2 – Are there _____ good supermarkets in your town?

   – Yes, there are, but _____ of them are very expensive.

3 – John never drinks beer. Have you got _____ other drinks for him?

4 – Are there _____ good restaurants near here?

   – There are _____ quite good restaurants in town, but there aren't _____ near here.

5 – Sorry, we haven't got _____ French wine, but we've got _____ good German wine. Would you like _____ German wine?

6 – Can I have _____ chips with my steak?

55

Unit 8 – Food and drink

5 Food

1 It is a green or yellow fruit.
2 You often start your meal with a . . . .
3 People often eat it in restaurants. The Americans and Argentineans are famous for it.
4 For most Germans Sunday lunch is not lunch without . . . .
5 People cannot live without it. You find it in all foods, and sometimes too much of it in soup!
6 It's a fruit. You often make juice out of it.
7 People often have it in their coffee.
8 It makes things sweet.
9 A lot of foreign people think that Germans eat them with every meal.

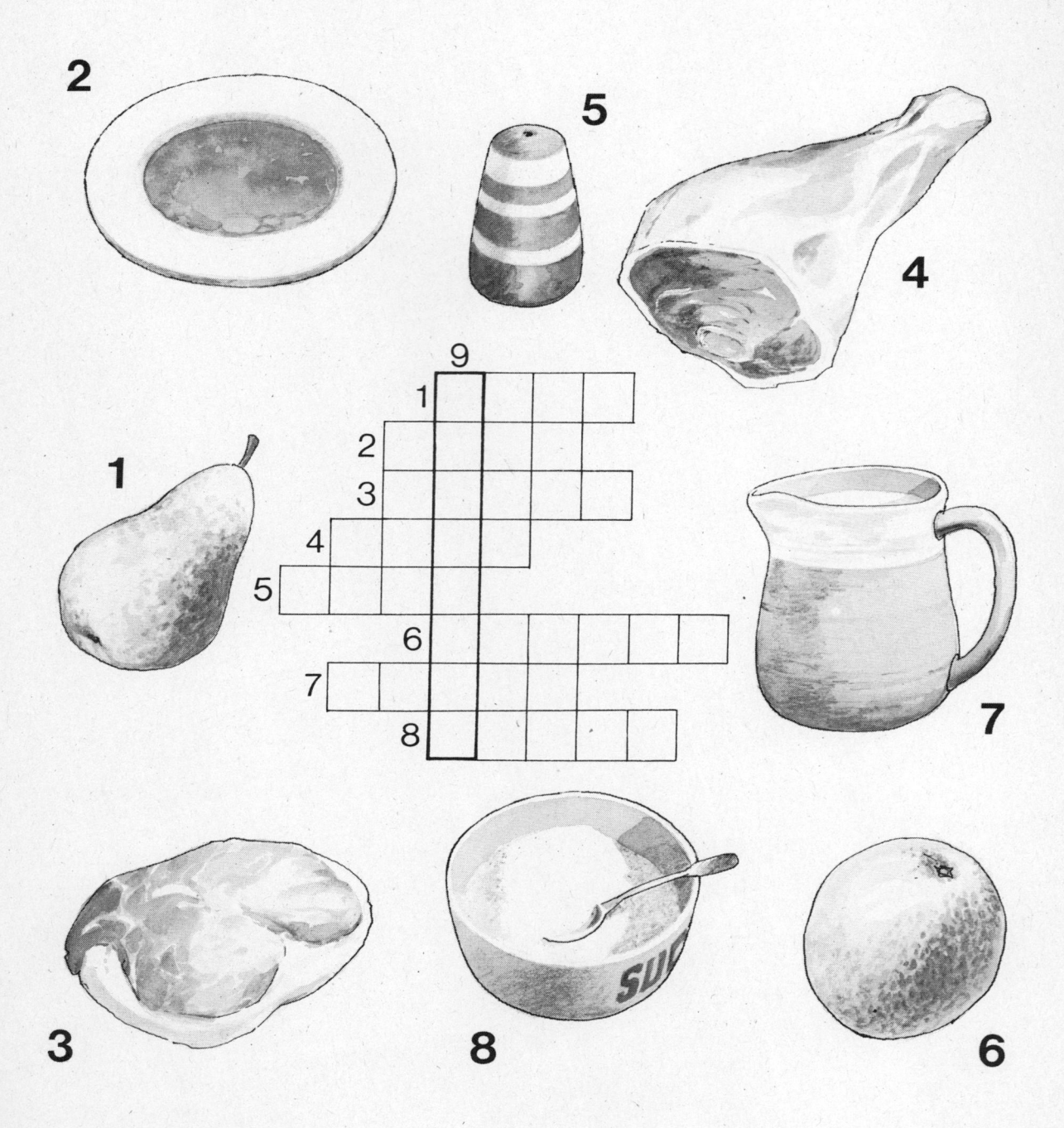

6 *Please hang this order on the outside of your door before 03.00 hrs.*

BEDROOM BREAKFAST ORDER

CONTINENTAL: £2 per person	No.	FULL ENGLISH: £4 per person	No.
Juices:			
Orange		**Juices:**	
Grapefruit		Orange	
Tomato		Grapefruit	
Coffee		Tomato	
Tea & Milk		Coffee	
Tea & Lemon		Tea & Milk	
Croissant ☐ Rolls ☐		Tea & Lemon	
Toast and Butter ☐		Croissants ☐ Rolls ☐	
Marmalade ☐		Toast and Butter ☐	
Honey ☐ Jam ☐		Marmalade ☐	
		Honey ☐ Jam ☐	
		Cornflakes	
		Rice Krispies	
No. of Persons: ☐ ROOM No: ☐		**Eggs:**	
		Boiled	
		Fried	
		Scrambled	
		Bacon	
		Sausage	
		Tomato	

Breakfast to be served between:

7.00 – 7.30 ☐   8.00 – 8.15 ☐   8.45 – 9.00 ☐
7.30 – 7.45 ☐   8.15 – 8.30 ☐   9.00 – 9.30 ☐
7.45 – 8.00 ☐   8.30 – 8.45 ☐   9.30 – 10.00 ☐

Signature ....

Stellen Sie sich ein Frühstück Ihrer Wahl zusammen.

Unit 8 – Food and drink

7 *Vervollständigen Sie den Briefausschnitt.*

Der Schreiber des Briefs hat morgens nicht viel Zeit und ißt deshalb nur eine Scheibe Brot und trinkt eine Tasse Kaffee. Um 10 Uhr ißt er ein Sandwich. Das Mittagessen nimmt er in der Kantine ein, wo er oft eine Suppe und Fleisch mit Kartoffeln ißt. Abends nimmt er keine warme Mahlzeit ein. Er ißt gewöhnlich Sandwiches und trinkt ein Glas Bier.

You ask me about what I eat every day. Well, _____, so _____ a slice*) of bread and _____ _____. At _____ sandwich. _____ _____ in the canteen where _____ _____ and some _____ with _____. _____ a hot _____. I usually _____ _____.
....

*) = Scheibe

Unit 9 Talking about the past

1 Wie man die Vergangenheit von regelmäßigen Verben bildet

*In dieser Übung kommen viele der **regelmäßigen Verben** vor, die Sie schon kennen. Sehen Sie sich die Bildungsregel in 1.1 des Lehrbuchs noch einmal an, und setzen Sie dann die Verben aus den Klammern in die richtige Form.*

This year I _____¹ (remember) my wife's birthday for the first time since (= seit) we _____² (live) in London. I _____³ (plan)ᵃ⁾ a surprise (= *Überraschungs-*) party and _____⁴ (invite) all our friends. I _____⁵ (ask) them not to tell my wife about the party, and they all _____⁶ (agree). But my wife _____⁷ (love) surprises, too, and she also _____⁸ (want) to plan a surprise party for her birthday. So she _____⁹ (invite) all her friends, – and their husbands, wives and friends . . .

It **was** a surprise party! It _____¹⁰ (start) at 8, and Betty _____¹¹ (mix) some cocktails while I _____¹² (open) some bottles of wine. We had a lot of beer but not so much wine, and it _____¹³ (seem) that most of our guests _____¹⁴ (prefer) wine. At nine o'clock I could see that we _____¹⁵ (need) more wine, so I _____¹⁶ (phone) our neighbour to ask him if he could help. He _____¹⁷ (recommend) a shop in the new shopping centre. He _____¹⁸ (remember) that they had some very good French wines.

I _____¹⁹ (walk) to the shopping centre. When I _____²⁰ (arrive) at the shop it was not open. I _____²¹ (try)ᵃ⁾ to find a taxi, but couldn't, so I _____²² (travel) to town by bus. One hour later, I _____²³ (arrive) at a wine shop that was open. I _____²⁴ (order) what I _____²⁵ (need), and then the shop assistant _____²⁶ (help) me to find a taxi. When I got back home, the party was over (= *war zuende*).

I _____²⁷ (watch) Betty as she _____²⁸ (wash) the dishes. I was glad that she wasn't angry (= *verärgert*). The next time, we _____²⁹ (agree), we would plan our surprise parties together (= *zusammen*)!

ᵃ⁾ planned; tried – Schreibregel in 2.2 des Lehrbuchs.

Unit 9 – Talking about the past

2 Wie man Ja/Nein-Fragen in der Vergangenheit stellt, und wie man auf solche Fragen antwortet

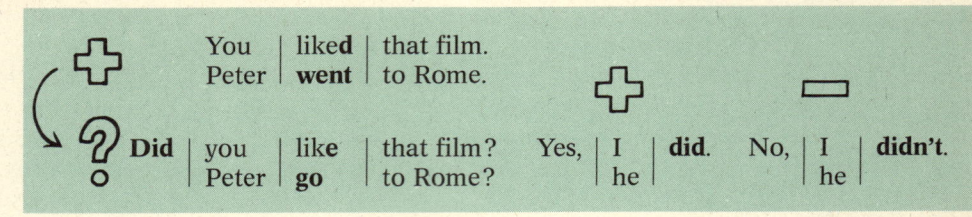

+	You / Peter	lik**ed** / **went**	that film. / to Rome.		+		–	
? **Did**	you / Peter	lik**e** / **go**	that film? / to Rome?	Yes,	I / he	**did**.	No, I / he	**didn't**.

Mr Brown is back from a business trip (= *Geschäftsreise*). He asks his assistant about last week:

Vervollständigen Sie die Fragen und Antworten.

1 – _____ Sheila write the letters to Brown & Sons? – Yes, _____.

2 – _____ Robinson & Co phone us last week? – No, _____.

3 – _____ the Germans order our new computer? – Yes, _____.

4 – _____ Maxwell agree with our plans (= *Pläne*) for Africa? – Yes, _____.

5 – _____ we get an answer from that firm in Australia? – No, _____.

6 – _____ you meet Ralf Nicolson at the airport? – Yes, _____.

3 Wie man die Vergangenheit von **be** bildet

I am	▷	I **was**
he/she/it is	▷	he/she/it **was**
we/you/they are	▷	we/you/they **were**

Setzen Sie die richtigen Formen von be ein.

1 A week ago, this TV _____ $280 and it _____ $249,95 now.

2 **Sale 19.99**
J. Reg. 23.99. Men's Paragon hi-top basketball shoe.

These basketball shoes _____ $23.99 and they _____ $19.99 now.

3 – The Johnsons _____ usually very nice people, but they _____ not very friendly yesterday.

4 – Sharon _____ in Italy last year and she _____ on holiday in Germany now.

5 – We _____ at home last weekend and we _____ at home this weekend. Why can't we go out and do something?

Unit 9 – Talking about the past

4 Wie man Vollverben in der Vergangenheit verneint

+		–
I worked	▷	I didn't (= did not) work
Peter went		Peter go

Setzen Sie die richtigen Vergangenheitsformen ein.

1 – I _____ (phone) Jennifer last week, but I _____ (not talk) to her husband.

2 – I _____ (read) the morning paper, but I _____ (not read) the sports news.

3 – She _____ (answer) my first question, but she _____ (not answer) my second question.

4 – They _____ (visit) Disneyworld, but they _____ (not visit) Cape Canaveral.

5 – Eric _____ (drink) a lot of beer at the party, but he _____ (not drink) wine.

5 Wie man die Äußerungen eines anderen kommentiert

Oh, really?   Did you?   That's nice.   That's interesting.   Oh, dear.

Kommentieren Sie die Äußerungen des Gesprächspartners.

1 – I'm planning to go to Australia and start a new life there.

   Sie fragen erstaunt, ob das wahr ist.

   – _____

2 – Jim has got a new girlfriend.

   Sie finden das interessant.

   – _____

3 – John helped me to paint my house.

   Sie finden das nett.

   – _____

4 – Angela is in hospital. She is very ill.

   Sie äußern erschreckt ihr Erstaunen.

   – _____

5 – I bought a new car.

   Sie fragen ungläubig nach.

   – _____

61

Unit 9 – Talking about the past

6 Wie man über etwas Vergangenes berichtet

Setzen Sie die richtigen Vergangenheitsformen ein.

From a letter by an American tourist to his family in Milwaukee:

We _____¹ (start) our sight-seeing tour at 8 o'clock and _____² (visit) the Tower of London where we _____³ (see) the famous Crown Jewels.ᵃ⁾ From there we _____⁴ (go) to Buckingham Palace where we _____⁵ (watch) the Changing of the Guard.ᵇ⁾ It _____⁶ (be) very interesting. After that we _____⁷ (have) something to eat in St. James's Park. In the afternoon the bus _____⁸ (take) us to Madame Tussaud's. At 6 p.m. we _____⁹ (meet) at Flanagan's and _____¹⁰ (have) a nice dinner. After dinner we _____¹¹ (drive) to Prince Edward's Theatre where we _____¹² (see) 'Evita'.ᶜ⁾ . . .

7 Wie man Fragen mit einleitenden Fragewörtern in der Vergangenheit stellt

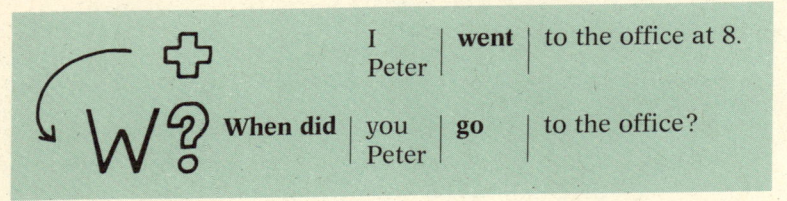

+	I / Peter	went	to the office at 8.
W?	When did	you / Peter	go	to the office?

Notebook:
- started trip at uuuu o'clock
- drove to uuuuu uuuuu
- after that visited uuuuuu uuu
- then travelled to uuuuuu
- ate lunch at the uuuuuuu uuuuuu
- swam in uuuuuu
- drank uuu glasses of beer at the Lakeside Pub
- got back to the hotel very late because uuu uuuu uuu

ᵃ⁾ *Kronjuwelen* ᵇ⁾ *Wachablösung* ᶜ⁾ *ein Musical*

Unit 9 – Talking about the past

Stellen Sie Fragen nach den unleserlichen Eintragungen.

1 When did you _____?
2 Where _____ to?
3 _____?
4 _____ to then?
5 _____?
6 _____?
7 _____
   _____?
8 _____?

8 Wie man ausdrückt, daß man sich nicht ganz sicher ist oder etwas nicht weiß

- About ... years ago.   - I (really) can't/don't remember when....   - I'm not sure, but I think....
- I'm afraid I don't know.   - I think it was/they were....

Try to answer these questions.

1 – Do you remember where the Olympic Games (= *Olympische Spiele*) were in 1968?
   – _____
   _____.

2 – When was the last time you saw a good film?
   – _____
   _____.

3 – Can you tell me when you got your first car?
   – _____
   _____.

4 – Do you still know when you got your first kiss?
   – _____
   _____.

5 – Do you know what presents you got for your last birthday?
   – _____

Unit 9 – Talking about the past

9 In den Buchstaben sind 17 Vergangenheitsformen versteckt.

Manche Vergangenheitsformen müssen waagerecht und andere senkrecht gelesen werden.

```
a n s w e r e d g
c u w s p e n t a
o v a w m a d e v
m i t a s a w a e
p s c s d p m e t
a i h h r a d i d
r t e e a i o m e
e e d d n n w a s
d d j u k t i o t
w e n t y e a d m
d r o v e d h a d
```

10 Fill in the **simple past forms** (= Vergangenheitsformen).

1 try   7 think
2 rob   8 sit
3 travel   9 write
4 plan   10 make
5 go   11 come
6 meet   12 drive

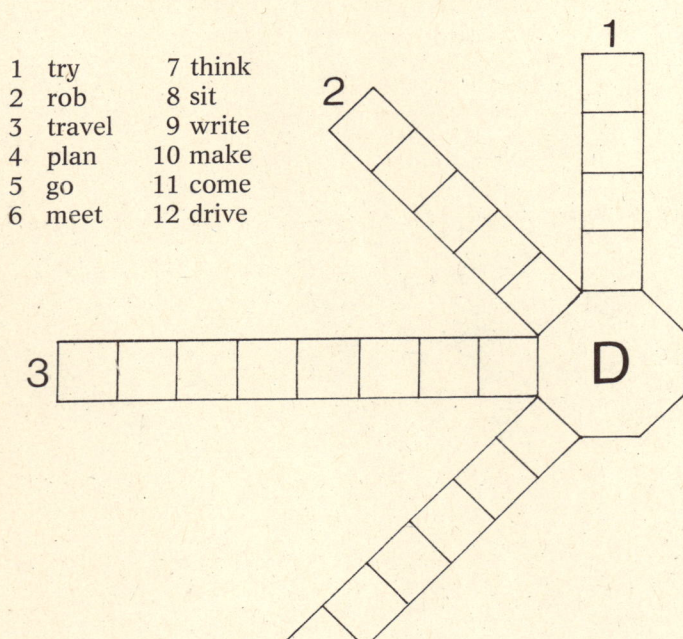

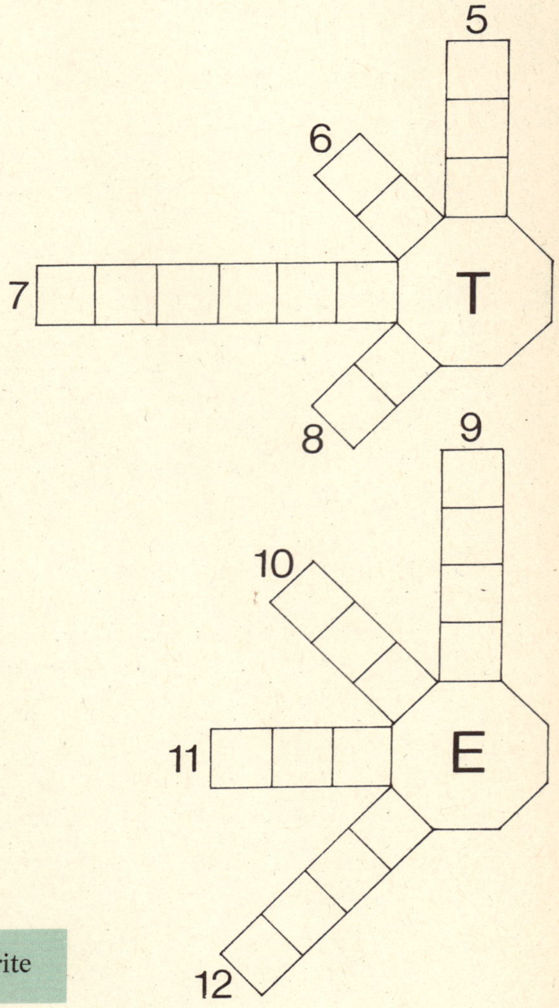

11 Fill in the right **simple past forms** of **these verbs**.

come, get, have, help, make (2 x), spend, be, watch, go, write

What my day _____ ¹ like yesterday.

– I _____ ² up at 7. I _____ ³ the breakfast for the family at 7.30. After that

I _____ ⁴ the beds. Then I _____ ⁵ an hour working in the garden.

At 10 o'clock I _____ ⁶ shopping. When I _____ ⁷ back home

I _____ ⁸ a letter to my mother. I _____ ⁹ lunch at 12.30 with Mary and Cathy.

In the afternoon I _____ ¹⁰ the children with their homework and in the evening

I _____ ¹¹ TV.

Can you write down what your day was like yesterday?

Unit 10 What's the matter?

1 Wie man auf die Frage nach dem Befinden antworten kann

| – How are you? | – Very well, thank you.
Fine, thank you. | } Wenn man sich wohlfühlt. |
| | – So-so, thanks
Not so bad, thanks.
Quite well, can't complain. | } Wenn man sich nicht ganz so wohlfühlt. |

Fill in the answers. Sometimes there is more than one possible answer.

1 – How are you?

– _____.

– Oh, what's the matter?

2 – How are you?

– _____. And how are you?

– I'm fine, too, thank you.

3 – How are you?

– _____.

– Hm. Anything wrong?

4 – How are you?

– _____.

– That's good to hear (= *hören*).

2 Wie man Aufforderungen, etwas zu tun oder nicht zu tun, ausdrückt

Fill in **should** *or* **shouldn't**.

You can say it like this, too.

1 – You _____ only take this medicine when the doctor tells you to.

2 – You _____ put (= *legen*) the medicine where children can't get it.

3 – You _____ take medicine out of a box (= *Schachtel*) that doesn't say what is in it.

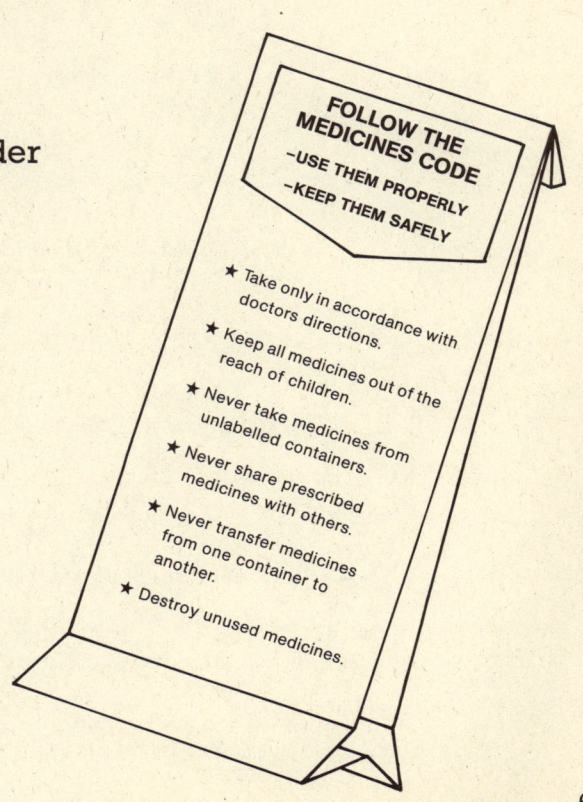

FOLLOW THE MEDICINES CODE
– USE THEM PROPERLY
– KEEP THEM SAFELY

★ Take only in accordance with doctors directions.
★ Keep all medicines out of the reach of children.
★ Never take medicines from unlabelled containers.
★ Never share prescribed medicines with others.
★ Never transfer medicines from one container to another.
★ Destroy unused medicines.

Unit 10 – What's the matter?

4 – You _____ take anyone else's tablets.

5 – You _____ put medicine from one box into another box.

6 – You _____ use up (= *verbrauchen*) all your medicine. If you don't use it up, you _____ destroy (= *vernichten*) it.

3   Wie man einen Befehl/eine Anweisung, etwas zu tun oder nicht zu tun, ausdrückt

– Go!   – **Don't** go!
– Stop!   – **Don't** stop!
– Do it!   – **Don't** do it!

*Setzen Sie **don't** nur dort ein, wo es notwendig ist.*

What the English teacher tells his/her students at night school.

– _____ [1] ask me if you don't understand a word.

– _____ [2] speak German, please.

– _____ [3] listen to the cassettes as often as possible.

– _____ [4] try to translate (= *übersetzen*) every English word.

– _____ [5] forget your homework.

– _____ [6] watch films in English or _____ [7] listen to radio programmes in English as often as possible.

– _____ [8] be afraid to make a mistake.

– _____ [9] learn the new words regularly.

– _____ [10] write too much down; it is better to use the time for speaking.

Unit 10 – What's the matter?

4 Wie man nach dem Zustand oder der Beschaffenheit fragt

> – What's/are ... like (today)?
> What was/were ... like (yesterday)?
> What will ... be like (tomorrow)?

Stellen Sie Fragen nach dem Zustand/der Beschaffenheit in der richtigen Zeit.

1 – _____ the weather _____ ? – It's raining again.

2 – _____ the weather _____ in England last summer? – It was warm and sunny.

3 – What _____ the weather _____ next weekend? – I think it will be cool and rainy.

4 – _____ these new cornflakes _____ ? – Oh, they are very good. We eat them every morning.

5 – _____ your summer holidays _____ ? – Wonderful. We had a lot of sun.

6 – _____ your new car _____ ? – It's a family car; it's very comfortable. Would you like to see it?

5 The Weather

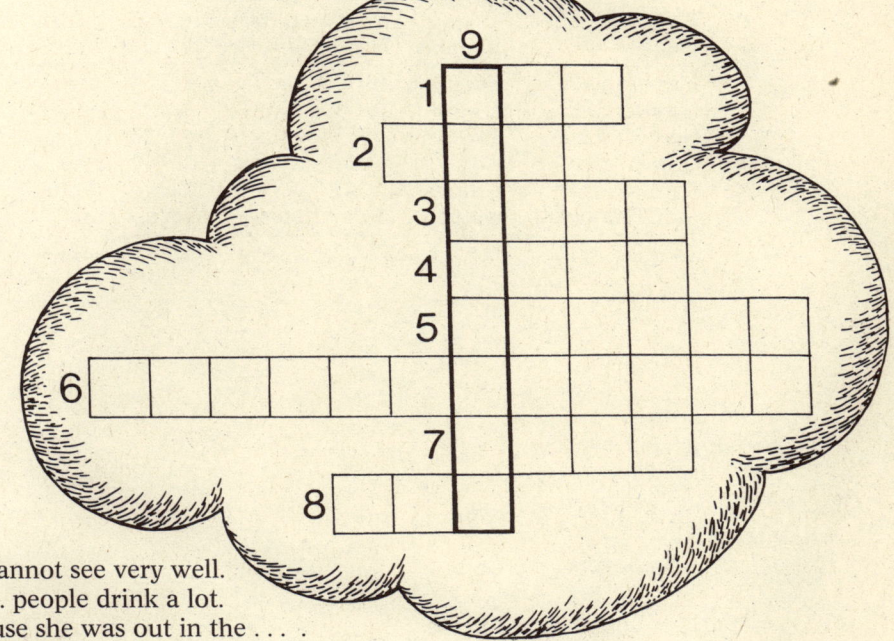

1 When there is ... you cannot see very well.
2 When the weather is ... people drink a lot.
3 Her coat was wet because she was out in the ... .
4 In the morning the sun is in the ... .
5 When it is ... you cannot see the sun.
6 In summer we sometimes have ... of more than 30°C in Scotland.
7 It is white and you often see it when it is very cold.
8 After the rain all my clothes were ... .
9 The weather ... tells you what the weather will be like tomorrow.

Unit 10 – What's the matter?

6

National Forecast

National temperatures

	Tuesday		Today		Thursday	
City	Wea	Lo/Hi	Wea	Lo/Hi	Wea	Lo/Hi
Atlanta	rain	46/75	ptcldy	52/70	tstrms	58/74
Atlantic City	cloudy	42/55	shwrs	41/58	shwrs	47/60
Boston	ptcldy	42/58	sunny	39/59	ptcldy	40/57
Chicago	tstrms	35/59	tstrms	47/58	shwrs	45/53
Dallas	ptcldy	62/84	tstrms	62/75	ptcldy	48/63
Denver	snoshw	30/33	snoshw	25/30	ptcldy	21/39
Los Angeles	sunny	48/62	sunny	47/64	sunny	49/66
Minneapolis	sunny	36/44	rain	34/42	cloudy	30/39
New Orleans	shwrs	56/78	ptcldy	63/80	ptcldy	63/73
New York	rain	43/56	sunny	40/60	rain	46/58
SaltLakeCity	sunny	37/46	windy	31/44	ptcldy	26/52
San Francisco	windy	39/58	sunny	48/59	fair	47/61
Seattle	fair	37/53	sunny	37/59	sunny	38/61

Data below recorded at 9 p.m. Tuesday

What is | showers (= shwrs) | in German? = _____

 | snowshower (= snoshw) | = _____

 | thunderstorms (= tstrms) | = _____

 | partly cloudy (= ptcldy) | = _____

Compare.

1 On Tuesday the weather in Boston was _____ (good) _____ the weather in Denver.

Unit 10 – What's the matter?

2 On Thursday it was _____ (cold) in Salt Lake City _____ in New Orleans.

3 On Thursday it was _____ (warm) in New York _____ on Tuesday.

SALT LAKE CITY   **LOS ANGELES**

Fill in the right words.

a On Tuesday it was _____ in Los Angeles.

b On Thursday there were _____ in Atlanta.

c On Wednesday there were _____ in Atlantic City.

7 *You are on holiday.*
Write a postcard to friends.
*Write about the **weather**,*
*the **food**, the **hotel***
*and the **prices**.*

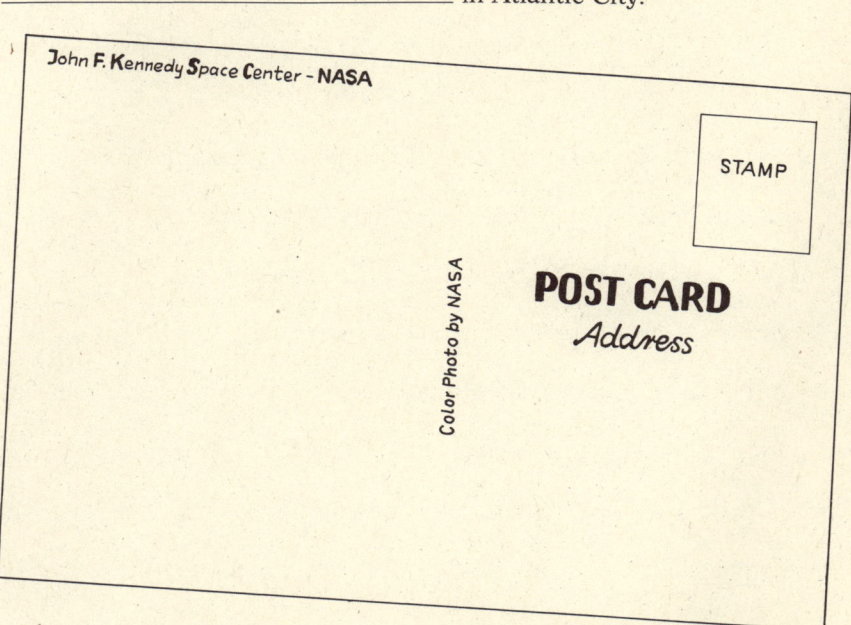

Stop Over   Test 2   (zu bearbeiten nach Unit 10)

Zur Arbeitsweise:

1 Versuchen Sie, die Testaufgaben zu lösen.
2 Überprüfen Sie Ihre Lösungen anhand des Schlüssels im Anhang des Arbeitsbuchs.
3 Wenn Sie Fehler gemacht haben,
   - schlagen Sie in dem Abschnitt in der Grammatikübersicht des Lehrbuchs nach, auf den verwiesen wird,
   - versuchen Sie dann noch einmal, die Aufgabe zu lösen.

1 *Fill in* **all, a lot of, any, anything, anybody, each, every, everybody, everything, some, something.**

1 John is a very friendly person. _____ in the street likes him.

2 You can ask him what you like, he has got an answer to _____.

3 _____ child of five has to go to school in England.

4 _____ of the three secretaries in our office can speak French.

5 _____ French people spend their holidays in foreign countries, but most stay in France.

6 – I haven't got _____ more stamps. Have you?

 – No, I haven't, but I can buy _____ for you when I go shopping.

7 I have got _____ friends, but only two really good friends.

8 – Would you like _____ to eat?

 – No, thank you. I can't eat _____ just now.

9 I don't feel very well. I don't want to talk to _____ now. Please ask him to go away.

Siehe Grammatikübersicht G 1(e)

2 *Setzen Sie die 2. Steigerungsstufe des Eigenschaftswortes ein.*

1 Jaguar, Porsche and Ferrari are all fast sports cars.

 Which is the _____?

2 Eric and Jim are good drivers, but Linda is the _____ driver of all.

3 A holiday in America is more expensive than a holiday in Spain, but a trip to Australia is the _____ holiday I know.

4 A Mercedes is more comfortable than most other cars, but most people think a Rolls-Royce is the _____ car.

Siehe Grammatikübersicht G 4(a)

3 *Vergleichen Sie.*

1 – Robert gets up at 8 a. m. and Lucy gets up at 7 a. m. Lucy _____
than Robert. (early)

2 – A room at the Garden Hotel costs £25 and a room at the Tower Hotel costs £15.

A room at the Tower Hotel _____
_____. (cheap)

3 – A bottle of French wine is £8 and a bottle of German wine is £8, too.

The bottle of French wine _____ just _____
_____. (expensive)

4 – I can play table tennis, but I can't play tennis. Tennis _____ not _____
_____. (easy)

5 – The pizza at Gino's isn't bad, but you should try the pizza at Tony's.

– The pizza at Tony's _____ even _____
_____. (good)

Siehe Grammatikübersicht G 4(b)

4 What they do in the evening

Bilden Sie Sätze; beachten Sie dabei die richtige Wortstellung.

1 Mr White – watch – always – the news on TV – at eight o'clock

_____.

2 After dinner – Mrs White – read the newspaper – usually

_____.

3 Colin – before dinner – often – go for a run – in the park

_____.

4 John – help – his neighbours – sometimes – in the garden

_____.

5 In the evening – often – Mr and Mrs White – a glass of wine – drink

_____.

Siehe Grammatikübersicht G 5(b), (c)

Stop Over – Test 2

5 *Setzen Sie die richtigen **Gegenwarts-** und **Vergangenheitsformen** von **be** ein.*

I	_am_ 1	very happy today, but I	_wasn't_ 6	happy yesterday.
you	_____ 2		you	_____ 7	
Lucy	_____ 3		she	_____ 8	
Peter and I	_____ 4		we	_____ 9	
The children	_____ 5		they	_____ 10	

Siehe Grammatikübersicht G 6.1(a)

6 *Setzen Sie die richtigen **Gegenwarts-** und **Vergangenheitsformen** ein.*

What Cynthia does every day.

What Cynthia did yesterday because she was late.

1 She _____ (get) up at 7.   She _____ up at 7.15.

2 She _____ (have) breakfast at 7.30.   She _____ breakfast at 7.45.

3 She _____ (take) the 8.15 bus.   She _____ the 8.30 bus.

4 She _____ (start) work at 8.30.   She _____ work at 8.45.

5 She _____ (drink) a cup of tea   She only _____ a cup of tea.
   and _____ (eat) a sandwich
   at 11 o'clock.

6 She _____ (go) home at 1 o'clock.   She _____ home at 1 o'clock, too.

Siehe Grammatikübersicht G 6.3(a), (b)

7 Things that are not true

Verneinen Sie die Verben; beachten Sie dabei die richtige Zeit.

1 – Mrs Dickens goes shopping every morning.

   – No, _____ shopping in the morning, she goes shopping in the afternoon.

2 – The Duponts are from England.

   – No, they _____ from England, they're from France.

3 – The Johnsons spent their last holidays in Italy.

   – No, they _____ their last holidays in Italy, that was two years ago.

4 – Peter and Mary like pop music.

   – No, they _____ pop music, they often listen to jazz music.

5 – Peter should take one of these tablets for his headache.

   – No, he _____ these tablets, they aren't for children.

Siehe Grammatikübersicht G 7(b)

Stop Over – Test 2

8 *Write down the questions.*

1 – _____ ?   – Well, I can read German, but I don't speak it.

– And what about your son? _____   – Yes, he does. He speaks two foreign languages.
_____ German?

2 – _____ your wife   – Yes, she did. She always goes to night school
_____   on Tuesday.
yesterday?

3 – _____ ?   – I live in an old house in Garden Street.

4 – _____ your husband   – I think he got home at 6, but I'm not sure.
_____ home yesterday?

5 – _____ do   – We played tennis with Claire and Duncan.
last weekend?

Siehe Grammatikübersicht G 7(c)

9 *Mit welchen Wörtern werden die Nebensätze eingeleitet?*

1 I didn't know . . . John speaks French.
2 In this picture Peggy is drinking a glass of wine
 . . . I am making dinner.
3 Harry always comes . . . help me when I need him.
4 Don't put the tablets on the table . . . the children
 can get them.
5 Roy always closes the windows . . . he goes out.
6 I can't wait . . . he comes. I have to go now.
7 I didn't like my teacher . . . I learned a lot from him.

Siehe Grammatikübersicht G 10

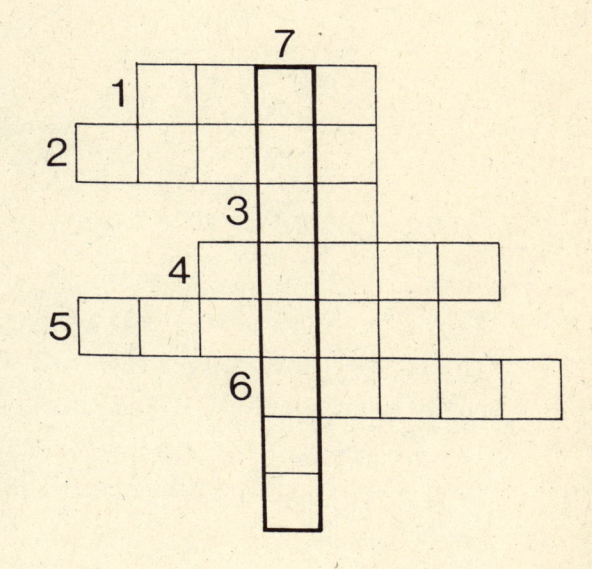

10 *Finden Sie die richtigen **Präpositionen**.*

1 – The supermarket is ten minutes from here . . . car.
2 – My hotel is . . . Victoria Station.
3 – It was cold from December . . . April.
4 – Is your wife . . . you?
5 – My car is that green one over there, . . . to the red sports car.
6 – Today is Wednesday, so the day . . . yesterday was Monday.
7 – I can't see Jim . . . all those people.
8 – There's an Intercity train . . . London and Inverness.

Siehe Grammatikübersicht G 13

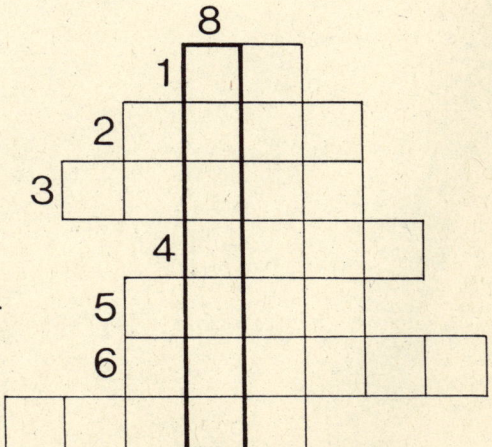

Stop Over – Test 2

11 *Schreiben Sie die Wörter in die richtige Spalte.*

a temperature, bread, carry, cheese, chicken, clean, cold, cook, cream, drive, eggs, happy, headaches, hot, housework, ill, lunch, potatoes, read, recommend, soup, sugar, swim, terrible, travel, wet, warm

What you can do	What you can eat	What you can feel

12 *Schreiben Sie in die richtige Spalte.*

hospitals – changing trains – going to famous places – quiet hotel rooms – eating their meals with salt – saying things twice – having a bath or a shower – drinking coffee for breakfast – listening to unpleasant news – sunny weather – travelling at night – headaches – waiting for a meal – feeling happy – sitting at the back of the theatre – eating a meal without a vegetable

What most people like	What most people don't like

Stop Over – Test 2

13 Questions

You can make ten questions out of these words.

~~What is~~ – you come – a post office near here – ~~Can you~~ – ~~your telephone number~~ – coffee or tea – What is – Would you like – are there in your town – How many supermarkets – to the cinema yesterday – Why can't – How much is it – Can I – in English money – have the menu, please – tell me – Did you go – how to get to the station – the weather like – Is there

1. *What is your telephone number?*
2. *Can you* _____
3. _____
4. _____
5. _____
6. _____
7. _____
8. _____
9. _____
10. _____

14 Happy holidays?

Henry and Pam are talking to their friend, John, about their summer holidays in France.

Unterstreichen Sie die richtigen Zeitformen.

John – Hello, Pam. Hello, Henry.

Henry and Pam – Hello, John.

John – | Do / Does / Did | you have a nice holiday?

Pam – Oh yes, thanks. We | swam / swim / are swimming | a lot and | playing / played / are playing | tennis with our French friends.

Henry – But it | wasn't / isn't / aren't | so nice in the evenings.

John – Oh? What did you | did / does / do | in the evenings?

75

Stop Over – Test 2

Henry – Well, we {am / was / were} all right, but our friends from Birmingham {have / had / has} one or two problems. Jean {wasn't / isn't / weren't} very happy, because Jack often went out without her.

Pam – So one night Jean {is going / goes / went} out to a disco, alone, too.

Henry – Jack never played tennis or {is swimming / goes swimming / went swimming} with us.

Pam – In the second week Jean didn't {talked / talk / talking} to Jack.

John – {Is / Does / Did} she talking to him now?

Henry – I {doesn't / didn't / don't} know, but I {saw / am seeing / sees} her next Saturday.

Schlüssel

Unit 0

1 1 – **What's your name**, please?
– Barker.
– And **what's your** first name, **please**?
– Anthony.

3 – **What's your name, please**?

2 – **I'm Mary.**   My name's Mary.
– **I'm Julie.** oder My name's Julie.
– **I'm Debbie.**   My name's Debbie.

4 – Hello. **I'm** Peter. **I'm** your **guide**.

2 1 that   2 this   3 this   4 That

3 1 d   2 c   3 b   4 a

4 1 – Hello, Tom! **How are you**?
– **I'm fine**, thank you. And **how are you**?
– Not **so bad**.
2 – Good morning, Mrs Brown.
– Good morning, Dave. **How are you**?
– **I'm fine, thank you**.
3 – Hi, Jack! **How are you** today?
– Oh, not **so bad**. And you?
– **Fine**, thanks.

5 1 b   2 a   3 a   4 a   5 b   6 a

6 1 Hello   2 Goodbye   3 What   4 teacher   5 girl   6 name   7 Lily   8 flower   9 your   10 How are you?

7 1 di**s**co   2 **c**owboy   3 **s**uper   4 **s**ouvenir   5 **f**arm   6 **h**elicopter   7 **l**ady   8 **o**kay   9 **t**eam   10 **s**how   11 **c**ornflakes

Unit 1

1 1 – **Where are** you **from**?
– **(I'm) from** Kuwait.

2 – **Where is** it **from**?
– **It's from** Ireland.

3 – **Where is** your friend **from**?
– Peter **is from** Bristol.

2 1 a – an   2 an – a   3 an – a   4 a – an – a

3 1 Yes, it is.   2 No, it isn't.   3 No, it isn't.   4 Yes, it is.   5 Yes, it is.
         No, it is not.   No, it is not.

4 a – **Are** you Pierre Jardin?
– No, **I'm** Peter Hummel.
– **Where are you** from, Peter?
– **I'm from** Freiburg in Germany,
  but **I live** in Hamburg now.
– **What's** your job?
– **I work** in a hotel.
  I'm a waiter.

b – **Are you** Maria?
– Yes, **I am**.
– **Where are you** from, Maria?
– **I'm** from Basel in Switzerland,
  but **I live** in Bern now.
– **Are you** a student?
– No, **I'm not**. **I'm** a secretary.
  I **work** in a hotel.

5 1 – How are you?   2 – How do you do?   3 – (Hello, Jack,) how are you?   4 – How are you?
5 – How do you do?

6 1 is – is – lives – works   2 'm – is – live/work – lives/works – work – works

7 1 friend**s** – flower**s**   2 live**s** – work**s**   3 name**s** – flower**s** – girl**s**   4 (Susan) work**s**
5 *Hier wird kein „s" hinzugefügt.*

Schlüssel

8 waagerecht: United States – Ireland – engineer – Irish – England
senkrecht: Australia – cowboy – waiter – housewife – secretary

10 **I'm** from **Munich**, and **I live** in **Frankfurt** now. **I work** in **a factory**. **Where are you** from? **What's your** job? . . . .

Unit 2

1 1 – **How many** shops **are there** in your village?
– **There are four**.

2 – **How many** hotels **are there** in your village?
– **There is (only) one**.

3 – **How many** supermarkets **are there** in your village?
– **There are two**.

4 – **How many** factories **are there** in your village?
– **There are none**.

2 1 My   2 Her   3 His   4 your   5 My

3 1 a   2 a/b   3 b   4 b   5 b   6 a   7 b   8 b   9 a

4 1 name of the town   2 guest's name   3 Mr Simpson's office   4 telephone number of the Westminster Bank   5 Peter's nationality   6 manager of the ABC Supermarket   7 Ann's room   8 Cindy's telephone number   9 directory of Oxford

5 4 four   14 fourteen   44 forty-four   5 five   15 fifteen   50 fifty   8 eight   18 eighteen   80 eighty
3 three   13 thirteen   30 thirty   9 nine   19 nineteen   90 ninety   99 ninety-nine

6 1 Their – There   2 There   3 Their   4 their   5 there   6 There – there

7 1 – Yes. Go straight ahead until you get to the second traffic-lights, then turn right and go along Green Street and it's on your right, opposite the bank.

2 – Yes. Go straight ahead until you get to the third traffic-lights, then turn right and go along King Street until you get to the second crossing, and the Rex is / it's on your left.

3 – Go straight ahead until you get to the second traffic-lights, then turn right and go along Green Street until you get to the second crossing, and it's on your right.

4 – Excuse me, can you tell me how to get to the Hilton Hotel, please?
– Yes. Go straight ahead until you get to the second traffic-lights, then turn right and go along Green Street until you get to the first crossing, then turn right and go along Market Street and the Hilton is/it's on your right.

8 1 telephone   2 address   3 floor   4 cinema   5 station   6 eight   7 traffic-lights   8 nine   9 six
10 eighty

9 1 Richman   2 caravan   3 hire   4 road   5 specialists   6 two   7 Brown   8 L. N.   9 sixteen
10 Maidstone

10 His **name** is Dr Betterton. **His address** is **48 Winstanley Road** and **his telephone number** is **(Sheerness)** 2734.

Unit 3

1 1 – This is nice.
2 – That's a nice/lovely dress.
3 – That's a nice/lovely building.
4 – This is lovely/nice.

2 1 you – you – your   2 his – I – he   3 we – our – our – He – his . . . I – my – They – They – their

Schlüssel

3 1 – Excuse me, where can we get coats, please?
2 – Excuse me, where can I get umbrellas, please?
3 – Excuse me, I'm looking for a pair of jeans. Where can I get jeans, please?

4 2 – Are these your records? – No, they aren't. Those are my records.
3 – Are these your keys? – No, they aren't. These are my keys.
4 – Is this your car? – No, it isn't. That's my car.

5 1 – **How much is this** home computer?
 – **It's £320**.

2 – **How much are these** three records?
 – **They're £2, £2.50 and £1.50./They're £6**.

3 – **How much are these** shoes?/**How much is this pair of** shoes?
 – They're £25.

4 – **How much is this camera**?
 – **It's £115**.

5 – **How much are these (two) T-shirts**?
 – **They're £2 and £3./They're £5**.

6 1 – You can't get telephone directories in a department store. (*oder* cannot)
2 – Can I have your umbrella, please?
3 – Your night school teacher can speak and write English.
4 – What can I get in that shop?
5 – Can you tell me where King Street is, please?
6 – We can get T-shirts in the department store in King Street. (*auch* can't/cannot)
7 – The bank can change notes for you.
8 – He can't wear that pullover, it's not his size. (*oder* cannot)

7 1 shoes 2 poster 3 film 4 camera 5 suitcase 6 coat 7 umbrella 8 pullover 9 blouse 10 trousers 11 dress 12 shirt 13 home computer

8 1 – I can see 2 shoes, a pair of trousers, a T-shirt and 4 socks.
2 – No, they aren't.
3 – They're white and blue.
4 – It's (an) American (T-shirt).
5 – It's $3.77.
6 – It's small.
7 – (One pair is) 88 ¢ (= cents).
8 – sparen
9 S (Small) = klein M (Medium) = mittelgroß L (Large) = groß

9 I like shopping in town, but things are very **expensive**. Jeans are from **80** Marks to **120** Marks. A **good pair of** shoes is 160 Marks. **How much are jeans** in your town?
And **how much is a good pair of shoes**?

Unit 4

1 1 – When is the restaurant open?
 – It's open from six o'clock in the evening till midnight.

2 – Is the Planetarium still open at five o'clock in the afternoon?
 – No, it isn't. It closes at half past four (in the afternoon).

3 – Is the bank still open?
 – No, it isn't. It closes at half past three (in the afternoon).

4 – When is the post office open in Dublin?
 – It's open from 8 o'clock (in the morning) till 11 o'clock at night.

Schlüssel

        5 – It's open from eight o'clock to twelve o'clock and from one o'clock to four o'clock.
        6 – It's open till six o'clock (in the evening).

2   19 : 45   a quarter to eight (in the evening)
     8 : 34   twenty-six minutes to nine (in the morning)
    11 : 29   twenty-nine minutes past eleven (in the morning)
    13 : 58   two minutes to two (in the afternoon)
    19 : 30   half past seven (in the evening)
    13 : 05   five minutes past one (in the afternoon)
    12 : 55   five minutes to one (in the afternoon)
     8 : 26   twenty-six minutes past eight (in the morning)
    11 : 31   twenty-nine minutes to twelve (in the morning)
     7 : 30   half past seven (in the morning)
    18 : 45   a quarter to seven (in the evening)
    14 : 02   two minutes past two (in the afternoon)

3   1 – What time are the trains to Inverness?
        – There's one at 8 a. m. and one at 12 a. m.

    2 – Is there a train to Inverness in the afternoon?
       – No, there isn't.

    3 – Is there a train to London in the morning?
       – (Yes, there is.) There's one at 8.30.

4   1 – .... **Shall we** go there on Sunday?
       – Not on Sunday. But **let's/we can** go there on Tuesday, when we've got more (= *mehr*) time.

    2 – **Shall we** buy her some flowers?
       – Yes, that's a good idea. **Let's** buy roses. ....
       – **Shall I** buy them ... ? ....

    3 – **Let's** go .... **We could/can** have ....
       – .... **Can/Could we** go ... **instead**? ....

    4 – **Shall we** go ... ?
       – Well, **I'm not really interested in** ....
       – **Let's** go to Madame Tussaud's **instead**.

5

	We write	We say
15/9/1941	15(th) September, 1941	the fifteenth of September, nineteen forty-one
23/11/1977	23(rd) November, 1977	the twenty-third of November, nineteen seventy-seven
1/3/1961	1(st) March, 1961	the first of March, nineteen sixty-one
22/2/1993	22(nd) February, 1993	the twenty-second of February, nineteen ninety-three
16/8/1854	16(th) August, 1854	the sixteenth of August, eighteen fifty-four
2/6/1999	2(nd) June, 1999	the second of June, nineteen ninety-nine

6a   1 – **Have you got** Kodak films?
        – I'm sorry, we **haven't got** Kodak films, but **we have got** Ilford films.

     2 – **Have you got** a brown T-shirt in size 42?
       – I'm sorry, **we haven't got** a brown T-shirt in your size, but **we have got** a nice red T-shirt.

     3 – **Have you got** Commodore home computers?
       – Well, **we have got** Commodore computers, but **we have** only **got** the Commodore 2000.

     4 – **Have you got** a good camera for £150?
       – Well, **we have got** one for £165; it's a very good camera from Japan.

6b   They've got Ilford films but they **haven't got** Kodak films. **They haven't got** a brown T-shirt in the right size but **they've got** a red T-shirt. **They've got** Commodore home computers, but **they've** only **got** the Commodore 2000. **They've got** a camera from Japan for £165.

Schlüssel

7 1 has got – hasn't got   2 have got – haven't   3 has ... got   4 have got – haven't got   5 has got
   6 have got – haven't got

8 1 her   2 him   3 you   4 us   5 them   6 you   7 you   8 you   9 me   10 you

9 waagerecht: March – Friday – time – evening – June – month – day – minute – Tuesday
   senkrecht: February – afternoon – p. m. – a. m. – morning

10 1 Night Sights – 1900 (7 p. m.) – £12.50
   2 City & Tower – 1400 (2 p. m.) – £6.70
   3 Westminster & Changing the Guard – 1000 (10 a. m.) – £5
   4 IN TOWN London Day Tour – 1000 (10 a. m.) – £12.70

11 I think **it is a good idea** to **come** by train. **Shall I meet you** at **the station**? **We can go** to Flanagan's and have dinner before we go home. . . . .

   Zeigen Sie Ihren Briefausschnitt Ihrem Kursleiter, wenn Sie Fragen haben.

Unit 5

1 1 – Would you like to come to my birthday party?
   2 – Would you like to go/come to the cinema with me?
   3 – Would you like to see my garden?
   4 – Would you like to listen to my Bob Dylan records?
   5 – Would you like to go/come to a pub with me and my friend?

2 1 are having – Are ... coming   2 am going – are ... going   3 are ... doing – am changing – am going   4 are working – are going   5 are selling – are buying

3 1 . . . **I'm having a party**, too.
   2 **We're sorry**, but **we're going to a concert**.
   3 . . . . **He's meeting a friend**.
   4 **I'm** sorry, but **I'm working** tonight.
   5 **We're** sorry, but **we're having guests**.

4 1 Janet: – Fred, **what are you doing** at the moment?
      Fred: – **Oh, nothing, really**.
      Janet: – I'm **working in the garden. Could you perhaps help** me?

   2 Angela: – **What are you doing** on Friday evening?
      Neighbours: – **Oh, nothing, really**.
      Angela: – I'd like to **go to the cinema. Could you perhaps** look after the baby?

   3 Roy: – What **are you doing** next **Saturday**?
      Janice: – **I'm going** on holiday **on Friday**.
      Roy: – Oh, **I'm having** my birthday party on **Saturday**. **It's a pity** you can't come.

5 Mrs Grey: – **Is** Paul **doing** his homework?
   Mr Grey: – No, **he isn't. He is/'s phoning** a friend.
   Mrs Grey: – Hm. **Is** Grandpa **watching** TV?
   Mr Grey: – Yes, **he is**. He **is/'s sitting** in his room.
   Mrs Grey: – **Are** Ann and Andrew **playing** with their computer?
   Mr Grey: – Yes, **they are**. And they **are listening** to records.
   Mrs Grey: – **Are** you **going** to night school tonight?
   Mr Grey: – No, **I'm** not.
   Mrs Grey: – **Are** we **having** dinner now?
   Mr Grey: – No, we **aren't**. We **are/'re having** pizza at Gino's.

6 Third floor: Mrs Grey **is helping her** son with **his** homework, and her daughter **is washing her** hair.

   Second floor: Mr and Mrs Smith **are listening to** records and **their** children **are playing**.

   First floor: The Johnsons **are having** a party and **their** daughter **is reading** comics.

   Ground floor: Cindy **is writing** letters and Roy and Tom **are watching a** video film.

Schlüssel

7 1 Peter is taking a picture of Susan.
2 The tourists are listening to the guide.
3 John and Sue are playing tennis.
4 You are learning English.
5 They are watching an interesting video.

1 ... a picture of Susan?
3 Are John and Sue playing tennis?
4 Are you learning English?

8 1 talking   2 taking   3 sitting   4 writing   5 leaving   6 planning   7 inviting   8 changing
9 phoning

9 1 wine   2 invite   3 ticket   4 late   5 hour   6 letters   7 summer   8 pictures   9 while
10 new   11 group   12 interesting

10 Dear Cindy,
Thank you very much for the invitation to your birthday party. I'm sorry, but we can't come.
We're going on holiday to Italy next Monday. . . . .

Test 1

1 1 you   2 I   3 you   4 my/our   5 his   6 They   7 Their   8 you   9 you   10 we   11 We   12 I
13 we   14 our   15 She

2a 1 me   2 them   3 us   4 him   5 her

2b 1 you   2 her   3 him   4 you   5 you

3 1 this – that   2 those   3 This – this   4 these – these

4 1 Who   2 What   3 How   4 When   5 Where   6 Which   7 Whose

5 1 an   2 an   3 an   4 an   5 a   6 an   7 a   8 an

6 1 house   2 village   3 minutes   4 city   5 children   6 girls   7 months   8 husband   9 office
10 children   11 things   12 shoes   13 dresses   14 blouses   15 stores   16 housewives

7 1 Mr Smith's garden   2 the colour of your car   3 guest's nationality   4 Men's shoes   5 the size of
that blouse   6 Girls' pullovers   7 address of the cinema   8 number of that building

8 1 are   2 m   3 is   4 m   5 is   6 Are   7 are   8 are   9 is   10 is   11 Are   12 are   13 m
14 is

9 1 has got – has not got   2 have got – have not got   3 have ... got   4 have got   5 has ... got

10 1 I've got   2 I haven't got   3 He's got   4 She hasn't got   5 They've got

11 – Hello, Fred. This **is** Peter Brown **speaking**.
– Hello, Peter. Where **are** you **phoning** from?
– **I'm phoning** from my hotel room. I'm at the Garden Hotel.
– Is your wife with you?
– No, she isn't. She's at home with Johnny. He**'s going** to school next week. What **are** you and Jane
doing at the moment?
– We**'re watching** TV.
– **I'm going** to the theatre tonight to see 'Evita' . . . ?
– Just a moment, please. The children **are coming** in and . . . .

12 1 No, you can't.   2 Yes, it has.   3 Yes, it is.   4 Yes, it is.   5 Yes, they have.   6 No, you can't.
7 No, they aren't.   8 Yes, I have./No, I haven't.

Schlüssel

13

Buildings	Jobs	Time
airport	engineer	afternoon
bank	guide	evening
cinema	hairdresser	holiday
department store	housewife	hour
factory	secretary	month
hospital	shop assistant	night
school	teacher	tomorrow
shop	waiter	tonight
station	waitress	week

What you can wear	What you can read	What you can do
coats	addresses	ask
jeans	letters	buy
shirts	magazines	play
shoes	names	sell
skirts	newspapers	take pictures
socks	numbers	watch
suits	postcards	work
trousers	telephone directories	write

14 1 ? 2 ? 3 . *oder* ! 4 ? 5 ? 6 ? 7 . 8 . 9 . 10 ? 11 ? 12 . 13 . *oder* ? *(wenn sich jemand am Telefon meldet)* 14 . 15 ? 16 . 17 . 18 ? 19 . 20 ?

Unit 6

1 1 I ... read the newspaper .... 2 I ... phone friends .... 3 I ... watch TV .... 4 I ... go to the cinema .... 5 I ... write a letter ....

Die Wörter **usually, always, sometimes, often** und die Zeiten **in the morning/afternoon/evening, at ... o'clock**, ... müssen Sie entsprechend Ihren eigenen Gewohnheiten einsetzen.

2
1 She sometimes listens to the radio.
2 She always goes to the bathroom.
3 She usually has a shower.
4 She usually has breakfast before 7.30.
5 She often reads the morning paper.
6 She always starts work at 8 o'clock.
7 She often makes a cup of tea in the office.

3 1 'm working   2 play – 'm going   3 go – going – are having   4 are washing   5 are watching – watch

4
1 Are you from England?/Are you English?
2 Have you got a lot of English books?
3 Can you speak German?
4 Are you good at sports?

5
1 Do you speak British or American English?
2 Do you like American cars?
3 Do you want to go on holiday to England?
4 Do you sometimes go to see English films?
5 Do you often read English books?
6 Do you drive a foreign car?

6 1 e   2 c   3 f   4 a   5 d   6 b   7 g

7
1 – **Do** John and Jennifer **live** in Croydon?
– **No, they don't.**

2 – **Do** they **work** on Saturdays?
– **No, they don't.**

Schlüssel

3 – **Does** Jennifer **speak** German?
– **Yes, she does.**

4 – **Do** John and Paul **speak** a foreign language?
– **No, they don't.**

5 – **Do** John, Paul and Jennifer **like** working with people?
– **Yes, they do.**

6 – **Does** Paul **live** in Croydon?
– **Yes, he does.**

7 – **Does** Jennifer **live** in Croydon, too?
– **No, she doesn't.**

8 – **Does** John **drive** an English car?
– **Yes, he does.**

9 – **Do** Paul and Jennifer **drive** French cars?
– **No, they don't.**

8 1 – Where do you work?
2 – How do you travel to work?
3 – When does Roger usually start work?
4 – What do your children do when you are at work?
5 – When does Roger usually get home?
6 – How often do you have dinner with your children?
7 – What do you think about your job?

9 1 I don't work   2 she doesn't like   3 I don't think   4 they don't get up   5 we ... don't work
6 I don't know

10 1 Congratulations!
2 I'm sorry to hear that./Oh dear!
3 Oh, good./ I'm glad to hear that.
4 Oh, how nice for you!
5 Oh dear! *(auch andere Möglichkeiten)*

11 1 every   2 first   3 news   4 all   5 passenger   6 to agree   7 every   8 more   9 to forget

12 2 What does she learn at night school?
3 Where does she sit the other evenings?
4 What does she read?
5 What does she (sometimes) play?

a ask   b tell   c go   d learn   e sit   f read   g watch   h play

Für den Briefausschnitt kann kein Schlüssel gegeben werden. Im Zweifelsfalle fragen Sie bitte Ihre/n Kursleiter/in.

Unit 7

1 1 I prefer the car on the right because it is more comfortable.
2 I prefer the dress on the left/right because it is smarter.
3 I prefer the book on the left/right because it is more interesting.
4 I prefer the suitcase on the right because it is bigger.

2 1 – I'd go by train because (I think) it's faster.
2 – You should buy a bigger pullover/one.
3 – I'd go to the film with Robert Redford because it's more interesting.
4 – You should buy a new car.

3 1 The first house is more comfortable than the second (one).
2 The second house is (just) as expensive as the third (one).
3 The first house is bigger than the third (one).

Schlüssel

    4 The second house is older than the third (one).
    5 The garden of the first house is bigger than the garden of the third (one).
    6 The first house is (just) as old as the third (one).

4 1 – I'm afraid I don't agree. I think (that) cars in Germany are more modern than cars in America.
        – *oder* – I think (that) cars in Germany are (just) as modern as cars in America.
    2 – I'm afraid I don't agree. I think (that) the Minimarket is more convenient than the Spar Market.
        – *oder* – I think (that) the Minimarket is (just) as convenient as the Spar Market.
    3 – I'm afraid I don't agree. I think (that) holidays in England are more expensive than holidays in Germany. – *oder* – I think (that) holidays in England are (just) as expensive as holidays in Germany.
    4 – I'm afraid I don't agree. I think (that) a plane/travelling by plane is safer than a train/travelling by train. – *oder* – I think (that) a plane/travelling by plane is (just) as safe as a train/travelling by train.

5 1 – Which is the best car?
    2 – Where is the cheapest supermarket?
    3 – Where is the most comfortable restaurant?
    4 – How much are the most expensive shoes?
    5 – Who is the nicest shop assistant?
    6 – Which is the most interesting film?
    7 – Which is the biggest building?

6 1 cheap   2 convenient   3 famous   4 fast   5 foreign   6 attractive   7 quiet   8 special   9 terrible   10 careful   11 interesting   12 comfortable

7 NAME   **Hans Schmidt**
    ADDRESS   **Karlstr. 5, 6 Frankfurt, Germany**
    Daytime Phone Number   **069/23794**
    Please reserve   **2**   rooms.

1st Room	B	2	
2nd Room	C		Maria (6)

Date of arrival: **16th Aug.**   No. of nights: **3**

Signed **Hans Schmidt**   Date: **(genügend lang vor der Ankunft)**

8 The Parkhotel is quieter than the Wiesenhotel because it is near a park and the Wiesenhotel is only two minutes from the station. The Wiesenhotel is not as comfortable as the Parkhotel, but it has got a radio in every room. The Parkhotel has got a TV in every room. A room with bath is as expensive in the Wiesenhotel as it is in the Parkhotel. It's 100 Marks. . . . .

Es gibt natürlich noch andere Möglichkeiten, diesen Briefausschnitt zu schreiben. Im Zweifelsfalle fragen Sie bitte Ihre/n Kursleiter/in.

Unit 8

1 1 Would you like   2 please   3 Would you like   4 please   5 can I have please
    6 what would you like   7 please   8 Would you like   9 please

2 – Waiter! **Can I have** the menu, **please**?
    – Just a moment, madam/sir.
    – **Can I** order now, **please**?
    – Yes, madam/sir. What would you like to start with?
    – **I'll have/take** a tomato soup.
    – And what would you like to follow?
    – **I'll have/take (the) steak with chips**.
    – Yes, madam/sir, steak with chips. And what would you like to drink?
    – Well, I think **I'll have** a glass of wine. What wine have you got?
    – We have some very good French and German wines.
    – **I'll have/ I'd like** a glass of French red wine.

85

Schlüssel

3 1 a 2 b 3 b 4 a 5 b 6 a 7 b

4 1 some – any – some 2 any – some 3 any 4 any – some – any 5 any – some – some 6 some

5 1 pear 2 soup 3 steak 4 meat 5 salt 6 orange 7 cream 8 sugar 9 potatoes

6 *Wenn Sie Fragen beim Ausfüllen der Bestelliste haben, besprechen Sie diese bitte mit Ihrem Kursleiter/ Ihrer Kursleiterin.*

7 You ask me about what I eat every day. Well, **I haven't got much time in the morning**, so **I only eat** a slice of bread and **drink a cup of coffee**. At **10 o'clock I eat a** sandwich. **I have lunch** in the canteen where **I often have soup** and some **meat** with **potatoes**. **In the evening I don't have** a hot **meal**. I usually **eat sandwiches and drink a glass of beer**. . . .

Unit 9

1 1 remembered 2 lived 3 planned 4 invited 5 asked 6 agreed 7 loved 8 wanted 9 invited
10 started 11 mixed 12 opened 13 seemed 14 preferred 15 needed 16 phoned
17 recommended 18 remembered 19 walked 20 arrived 21 tried 22 travelled 23 arrived
24 ordered 25 needed 26 helped 27 watched 28 washed 29 agreed

2 1 – Did . . . ? – . . . , she did.
   2 – Did . . . ? – . . . , they didn't.
   3 – Did . . . ? – . . . , they did.
   4 – Did . . . ? – . . . , he did.
   5 – Did . . . ? – . . . , we didn't.
   6 – Did . . . ? – . . . , I did.

3 1 was – is 2 were – are 3 are – were 4 was – is 5 were – are

4 1 phoned – did not talk 2 read – did not read 3 answered – did not answer 4 visited – did not visit
5 drank – did not drink

5 1 Oh, really? 2 That's interesting. 3 That's nice. 4 Oh, dear. 5 Did you?

6 1 started 2 visited 3 saw 4 went 5 watched 6 was 7 had 8 took 9 met 10 had
11 drove 12 saw

7 1 When did you start your trip?
   2 Where did you drive to?
   3 Who/What did you visit after that?
   4 Where did you travel to then?
   5 When/Where did you eat lunch?
   6 Where did you swim?
   7 How many glasses of beer did you drink at the Lakeside Pub?
   8 Why did you get back to the hotel very late?

8 *Hier kann kein Schlüssel gegeben werden. Im Zweifelsfalle fragen Sie bitte Ihre/n Kursleiter/in.*

9 waagerecht: answered – spent – made – saw – met – did – was – went – drove – had

   senkrecht: compared – visited – watched – washed – drank – painted – gave

10 1 tried 2 robbed 3 travelled 4 planned 5 went 6 met 7 thought 8 sat 9 wrote
10 made 11 came 12 drove

11 1 was 2 got 3 made 4 made 5 spent 6 went 7 came 8 wrote 9 had 10 helped
11 watched

Bei der Schreibaufgabe kann kein Schlüssel gegeben werden. Im Zweifelsfalle fragen Sie bitte Ihre/n Kursleiter/in.

Schlüssel

Unit 10

1 1 – So-so, thanks.
2 – Fine, thank you./ Very well, thank you.
3 – Quite well, can't complain./ Not so bad, thanks./ So-so, thanks.
4 – Very well, thank you./Fine, thank you.

2 1 should   2 should   3 shouldn't   4 shouldn't   5 shouldn't   6 should – should

3 1 –   2 Don't   3 –   4 Don't   5 Don't   6 –   7 –   8 Don't   9 –   10 Don't

4 1 **What's** the weather **like**?
2 **What was** the weather **like** in England last summer?
3 **What will** the weather **be like** next weekend?
4 **What are** these new cornflakes **like**?
5 **What were** your summer holidays **like**?
6 **What's** your new car **like**?

5 1 fog   2 hot   3 rain   4 east   5 cloudy   6 temperatures   7 snow   8 wet   9 forecast

6 showers   = Schauer
snowshowers = Schneeschauer
thunderstorms = Gewitter
partly cloudy   = teilweise bewölkt

 1 ... better than ...   2 ... colder ... than ...   3 ... warmer ... than ...

 a warm   b thunderstorms   c showers

7 The weather is lovely and it is very warm. The food is very good, too – we love the pizza. The hotel is very comfortable. We have got a colour TV in our room. It's very nice here, but things are just as expensive as in Germany.

Zeigen Sie Ihre „Postkarte" Ihrer Kursleiterin/Ihrem Kursleiter; sie/er wird Ihnen mögliche Verbesserungsvorschläge machen.

Test 2

1 1 Everybody   2 everything   3 Every   4 Each   5 A lot of   6 any – some   7 a lot of
8 something – anything   9 anybody

2 1 fastest   2 best   3 most expensive   4 most comfortable

3 1 ... gets up earlier ....   2 ... is cheaper than a room at the Garden Hotel.   3 ... is just as expensive as the bottle of German wine.   4 ... is not as easy as table tennis.   5 ... is even better than the pizza at Gino's.

4 1 (At eight o'clock) Mr White always watches the news on TV (at eight o'clock).
2 (After dinner) Mrs White usually reads the newspaper (after dinner).
3 (Before dinner) Colin often goes for a run in the park (before dinner).
4 John sometimes helps his neighbours in the garden.
5 (In the evening) Mr and Mrs White often drink a glass of wine (in the evening).

5 1 am   2 are   3 is   4 are   5 are   6 wasn't   7 weren't   8 wasn't   9 weren't   10 weren't

6 1 gets – got   2 has – had   3 takes – took   4 starts – started   5 drinks – eats – drank   6 goes – went

7 1 she does not go/ doesn't go   2 are not/ aren't   3 did not spend/ didn't spend   4 do not like/ don't like   5 should not take/ shouldn't take

8 1 Do you speak German? ... ? Does he speak ... ?
2 Did ... go to night school ... ?
3 Where do you live?
4 When/What time did ... get ... ?
5 What did you ... ?

87

Schlüssel

9   1 that   2 while   3 to   4 where   5 before   6 until   7 although

10   1 by   2 near   3 until   4 with   5 next   6 before   7 among   8 between

11

What you can do	What you can eat	What you can feel
carry	bread	a temperature
clean	cheese	cold
cook	chicken	happy
drive	cream	headaches
housework	eggs	hot
read	lunch	ill
recommend	potatoes	terrible
swim	soup	wet
travel	sugar	warm

12

What most people like:	What most people don't like:
going to famous places	hospitals
quiet hotel rooms	changing trains
eating their meal with salt	saying things twice
having a bath or a shower	listening to unpleasant news
drinking coffee for breakfast	travelling at night
sunny weather	headaches
feeling happy	waiting for a meal
	sitting at the back of the theatre
	eating a meal without a vegetable

13
1 What is your telephone number?
2 Can you tell me how to get to the station?
3 What is the weather like?
4 Would you like coffee or tea?
5 How many supermarkets are there in your town?
6 Why can't you come?
7 How much is it in English money?
8 Can I have the menu, please?
9 Did you go to the cinema yesterday?
10 Is there a post office near here?

14
John – Hello, Pam! Hello, Henry!
Henry – Hello, John.
and
Pam
John – **Did** you . . . ?
Pam – Oh yes, thanks! We **swam** a lot and **played** . . . .
Henry – But it **wasn't** so nice in the evenings.
John – Oh? What did you **do** in the evenings?
Henry – Well, we **were** . . . , . . . Birmingham **had** . . . . Jean **wasn't** . . . .
Pam – So one night Jean **went** . . . .
Henry – Jack never played tennis or **went swimming** with us.
Pam – In the second week Jean didn't **talk** to Jack.
John – **Is** she talking to him now?
Henry – I **don't** know, but I **am seeing** . . . .

Inhaltsverzeichnis der Übungsinhalte

Lehrbuchbezug: zu bearbeiten nach Durchnahme von		Übungsinhalte	Seite
1.2	Unit 0	1 Wie man seinen Namen sagt und nach Namen fragt	1
1.3		2 Wie man *this* und *that* benutzt	2
2.2		3 Wie man jemanden begrüßt	2
2.5		4 Wie man sich nach dem Befinden erkundigt, und wie man auf solche Fragen antwortet	3
2.5		5 Wie man *am*, *are* und *is* benutzen kann	3
nach Unit 0		6 Vokabelrätsel	4
nach Unit 0		7 Rätsel zu englischen Wörtern, die auch im Deutschen benutzt werden	4
2.3	Unit 1	1 Wie man nach der Herkunft fragt, und wie man auf solche Fragen antwortet	5
2.4		2 *A* oder *an*?	5
2.4		3 Wie man auf *Ja/Nein-Fragen* antwortet	6
4.2		4 Wie man Auskünfte über sich selbst gibt	6
5.2		5 Wie man nach dem Befinden fragt, und was man bei einer förmlichen Vorstellung sagt	7
5.3		6 Wie man Informationen über sich bzw. eine andere Person weitergibt	7
5.3		7 Wo man die s-Endung benutzt	8
nach Unit 1		8 Vokabelrätsel: Länder, Nationalitäten und Berufe	8
nach Unit 1		9 Leseverständnisübung: Ausfüllen eines Anmeldeformulars	8
nach Unit 1		10 Schreibaufgabe: Ausfüllen eines Briefausschnitts	8
1.2	Unit 2	1 Wie man nach der Anzahl fragt	9
1.4		2 Wie man Zugehörigkeit ausdrückt	9
1.6		3 Was man am Anfang eines Telefongesprächs sagt	9
1.8		4 Wie man die Zugehörigkeit zu einer Person und einer Sache bezeichnet	10
2.2		5 Wie man Zahlen schreibt	10
3.2		6 Wie man *there* und *their* benutzt	11
5.4		7 Wie man Auskunft auf die Frage nach dem Weg gibt	11
nach Unit 2		8 Wortschatzrätsel	12
nach Unit 2		9 Leseverständnisübung: Anzeige einer Autovermietung	13
nach Unit 2		10 Schreibaufgabe: Vervollständigung einer Notiz	14
2.2	Unit 3	1 Wie man ausdrückt, ob einem etwas gefällt	15
4.2		2 Wie man Zugehörigkeit zu Personen ausdrückt	15
4.2		3 Wie man fragt, wo man etwas bekommt	16
5.3		4 Wie man Näheres und Ferneres bezeichnet	17
6.2		5 Wie man nach dem Preis fragt und darauf antwortet	18
6.3		6 Wie man *can* benutzen kann	19
nach Unit 3		7 Wortschatzrätsel: Things you can buy in a department store	20
nach Unit 3		8 Leseverständnisübung: Ausschnitte aus einem Kaufhauskatalog	21
nach Unit 3		9 Schreibaufgabe: Vervollständigung eines Briefausschnitts	21
1.4	Unit 4	1 Wie man nach Öffnungszeiten fragt, und wie man auf solche Fragen antwortet	22
2.2		2 Wie man sagt, wie spät es ist	23

Inhaltsverzeichnis der Übungsinhalte

Lehrbuchbezug: zu bearbeiten nach Durchnahme von		Übungsinhalte	Seite
2.4		3 Wie man nach Abfahrts- und Ankunftszeiten fragt, und wie man auf solche Fragen antwortet	24
3		4 Wie man Vorschläge macht, und wie man auf Vorschläge reagiert	24
4.2		5 Wie man das englische Datum schreibt und sagt	25
5.2		6 (a) Wie man fragt, ob jemand etwas hat, und wie man auf solche Fragen antwortet	26
5.2		(b) Wie man sagt, was jemand hat/nicht hat	27
5.2		7 Wie man sagt, was jemand hat/nicht hat	27
5.2		8 Wie man ausdrückt, für wen etwas bestimmt ist	28
nach Unit 4		9 Vokabelsuchspiel: Time and date	28
nach Unit 4		10 Leseverständnisübung: London Transport Guided Tours	28
nach Unit 4		11 Schreibaufgabe: Vervollständigung eines Briefausschnitts	30
1.2	Unit 5	1 Wie man jemanden einlädt	31
2.4		2 Wie man etwas ausdrückt, was gerade oder in naher Zukunft geschieht	31
2.4		3 Wie man die Ablehnung einer Einladung begründet	32
2.5		4 Wie man Einladungen oder Bitten um Hilfe einleiten, und wie man darauf antworten kann	32
3.1		5 Wie man fragt, ob jemand etwas gerade/in naher Zukunft macht, und wie man auf solche Fragen antwortet	33
3.1		6 Wie man beschreibt, was Leute gerade machen	34
3.1		7 Wie man Aussage- und Fragesätze im *Present Progressive* bildet	35
3.2		8 Wie man -ing-Formen von Verben schreibt	35
nach Unit 5		9 Wortschatzrätsel zu den Wörtern aus Unit 5	36
nach Unit 5		10 Schreiben eines Antwortbriefs	36
1.2	Unit 6	1 Wie ich sage, was ich regelmäßig tue	42
1.3		2 Wie man sagt, was jemand regelmäßig tut	42
1.5		3 Wie man regelmäßig wiederkehrendes Geschehen, und wie man augenblickliches oder zukünftiges Geschehen beschreibt	43
2.1		4 Wie man Fragen mit *Hilfsverben* stellt	44
2.1		5 Wie man Fragen mit *Do + Vollverb* stellt	44
2.2		6 Wie man auf *Ja/Nein-Fragen* antwortet	44
2.4		7 Wie man Fragen mit *do, does* stellt und darauf antwortet	45
3.2		8 Wie man Fragen mit einleitenden Fragewörtern stellt	46
4.2		9 Wie man Vollverben verneint	46
4.2		10 Wie man Bedauern und Mitgefühl ausdrückt oder, daß man sich mit jemandem freut	47
nach Unit 6		11 Wortschatzübung	47
nach Unit 6		12 Frageübung; Schreibaufgabe: Beschreibung von Hobbies und Freizeitbeschäftigungen	48
2.2	Unit 7	1 Wie man Vorlieben begründet	49
2.4		2 Wie man Ratschläge gibt	50
3.1		3 Wie man Vergleiche anstellt	51
3.2		4 Wie man Widerspruch ausdrückt	52
3.3		5 Wie man Eigenschaftswörter steigert	52
nach Unit 7		6 Wortschatzübung: Adjectives	53
nach Unit 7		7 Leseverständnisübung: Buchungsformular	53
nach Unit 7		8 Schreiben eines Briefausschnitts nach Stichwörtern	53

Inhaltsverzeichnis der Übungsinhalte

Lehrbuchbezug: zu bearbeiten nach Durchnahme von		Übungsinhalte	Seite
1.2	Unit 8	1 Wie man beim Frühstück etwas bestellt	54
2.3		2 Wie man ein Essen bestellt	54
3.2		3 Wie man *some* benutzt	55
5.2		4 Wie man *any* und *some* benutzt	55
nach Unit 8		5 Wortschatzrätsel: Food	56
nach Unit 8		6 Leseverständnisübung: Bestelliste für ein Hotelfrühstück	57
nach Unit 8		7 Vervollständigung eines Briefausschnitts über Eßgewohnheiten	58
1.1	Unit 9	1 Wie man die Vergangenheit von regelmäßigen Verben bildet	59
1.3		2 Wie man Ja/Nein-Fragen in der Vergangenheit stellt, und wie man auf solche Fragen antwortet	60
2.2		3 Wie man die Vergangenheit von *be* bildet	60
3.1		4 Wie man Vollverben in der Vergangenheit verneint	61
3.1		5 Wie man die Äußerung eines anderen kommentiert	61
3.2		6 Wie man über etwas Vergangenes berichtet	62
4		7 Wie man Fragen mit einleitenden Fragewörtern in der Vergangenheit stellt	62
4		8 Wie man ausdrückt, daß man sich nicht ganz sicher ist oder etwas nicht weiß	63
nach Unit 9		9 Rätsel zu Vergangenheitsformen	64
nach Unit 9		10 Rätsel zu Vergangenheitsformen	64
nach Unit 9		11 Schreibaufgabe: Tagesablauf	64
1.2	Unit 10	1 Wie man auf die Frage nach dem Befinden antworten kann	65
2.2		2 Wie man Aufforderungen, etwas zu tun oder nicht zu tun, ausdrückt	65
3.1		3 Wie man einen Befehl/eine Anweisung, etwas zu tun oder nicht zu tun, ausdrückt	66
4.3		4 Wie man nach dem Zustand oder der Beschaffenheit fragt	67
nach Unit 10		5 Wortschatzrätsel: The Weather	67
nach Unit 10		6 Leseverständnisübung: Wetterkarte der USA	68
nach Unit 10		7 Schreibaufgabe: Urlaubspostkarte	69

Verfasser	Willibald Bliemel
	Anthony Fitzpatrick
	Prof. Dr. Jürgen Quetz
Verlagsredaktion	Dr. Blanca-Maria Rudhart
Umschlag	Atelier Noth & Hauer, Berlin
Zeichnungen	Linden Artists (Valerie Sangster, Jon Davis), London; Gabriele Heinisch, Berlin
Fotos	British Tourist Authority, London (S. 25, 62); David Graham, Hewett Street Studios, London (S. 51, 66); USIS Press & Publication Service (S. 69)

Zu dem Lehrwerk TAKE OFF. Ein Englischkurs für Erwachsene, Band 1 sind außerdem für Kursteilnehmer/innen erhältlich:

Lehrbuch	Bestellnummer 48993
2 Übungscassetten mit Textheft	Bestellnummer 49043
1 Höraufgaben-Cassette	Bestellnummer 49027

1. Auflage
9. 8.
1992 91 | Die letzten Ziffern bezeichnen Zahl und Jahr des Druckes.

Alle Drucke dieser Auflage können, weil untereinander unverändert, im Unterricht nebeneinander verwendet werden.

Bestellnummer 49000

© Cornelsen & Oxford University Press GmbH, Berlin, 1985
Das Werk und seine Teile sind urheberrechtlich geschützt. Jede Verwertung in anderen als den gesetzlich zugelassenen Fällen bedarf deshalb der vorherigen schriftlichen Einwilligung des Verlages.

Satz	Fotosatz Gleißberg & Wittstock, Berlin
Druck	Klugedruck, Berlin
Weiterverarbeitung	Herbert Hensch, Berlin
	ISBN 3-8109-4900-0
Vertrieb	Cornelsen Verlagsgesellschaft, Bielefeld